Strategic
Risk
Management

Strategic Risk Management

How
Global Corporations
Manage Financial
Risk for
**Competitive
Advantage**

An Institutional Investor Publication

Mark J. Ahn

William D. Falloon

PROBUS PUBLISHING COMPANY
Chicago, Illinois

For Rhonda and Brittany
—MJA

For Juliana and Elena Ruth
—WDF

Contents

Acknowledgements

I would like to thank my colleagues at FMC Corporation, especially in the Trade Development and International Finance department, for providing a challenging learning environment. I would especially like to acknowledge Francisco G. Acevedo, who taught me the neurotic nature of capital markets and a healthy disregard for the status quo.

—MJA

This book is an expression of my deepest gratitude for my first editor, John G. Powers, who for five years pulled me through the mud when I was a heavy load. Thanks, John. Close on his heels, I thank all of my colleagues and friends at *Corporate Risk Management*, and the financial risk managers within this book who so freely shared their insights and time.

—WDF

Preface

Over the last two years, the idea that a corporate treasury operation in the U.S. could manage financial risks strategically has weathered the rhetorical highs and lows of a brooding debate. While many blue-chip companies such as Eastman Kodak, FMC Corp., Merck & Co., Sara Lee Corp., and the Walt Disney Co., to name a few, have initiated specific transactions or overall hedging strategies designed to protect them against significant changes in currency exchange rates, regulators such as the Securities and Exchange Commission (SEC) and policy makers such as the Emerging Issues Task Force (EITF) of the Financial Accounting Standards Board (FASB) have at one time or another cast a cloud of confusion over the legitimacy of pursuing such strategies.

The most significant diatribe came soon after an EITF meeting on August 10, 1989. At that meeting, the appropriateness of hedge accounting was called into question for hedges covering the foreign currency risk of future net income of a subsidiary whose transactions are denominated in its functional currency (which is not the parent's reporting currency). The SEC staff argued that hedge accounting requires identifying specific transactions, assets, or liabilities to be hedged; and, therefore, that hedging net income was inappropriate.

Furthermore, the SEC was also asked whether hedge accounting could be appropriate for financial instruments designated as a hedge of a percentage of estimated future revenues or costs. The SEC staff stated that a foreign subsidiary's future revenues or costs denominated in that subsidiary's functional currency do not expose either the subsidiary or the parent to foreign currency risk capable of being hedged for accounting purposes. Therefore, the SEC staff argued that hedge accounting would be inappropriate.

Adding to the controversy in the months that followed, the SEC Observer stated that the Office of the Chief Accountant received inquires requesting the SEC staff's position on the appropriate hedge accounting for foreign currency options that do not qualify for hedge accounting. The SEC staff stated that consistent with the guidance available in the AICPA Accounting Standards Executive Committee Issues Paper No. 86-2, *Accounting for Options*, and FASB Statement No. 52, *Foreign Currency Translation*, foreign currency options that do not qualify for hedge accounting should be accounted for at market value.

The potential assymetric problem of marking-to-market hedges of underlying exposures and of injecting dramatic profit and loss swings into their reported earnings was potentially enough to scare many corporations away from pursuing risk management strategies they believed made economic sense. To make a long story short, they felt that such interpretations were potentially throwing the baby out with the bath water—particularly those who were hedging long-term "economic" currency exposures related to overseas revenues or costs. Letters such as the one sent by Mentor Graphics condemning the SEC's position on this issue soon followed and continued all the way up to an EITF meeting on November 8, 1990, in which the issue of hedging anticipated exposures to currency risk was revisited (See Exhibits 1 and 2).

For most economic hedgers, this second meeting on November 8 was a positive step in the right direction that could help mend some of the fault lines they perceive between accounting conventions and economic reality. At the meeting, the EITF placed hedging through the use of currency options firmly under FASB 80 and AICPA Accounting Standards Executive Committee Issues Paper No. 86-2, both of which allow for favorable accounting treatment of anticipatory hedges, unlike FASB 52.

While this was certainly a technical victory for economic and strategic risk managers, it remains a difficult task at many corporations to persuade senior management to hedge at all, much less over time periods of two to five—or even 10 years. No doubt the issue of managing economic or strategic exposures—whether they be currency, interest rate or commodity-price risks—will continue to be debated in corporate boardrooms and among accountants and regulators.

Corporations face both long-term economic risk and short-term transaction risk. Combined, they represent a strategic risk—the risk a company faces as price volatility creates gains or losses in the future value of cash flows. These cash flow changes are caused by movements in interest rates, foreign exchange rates, or commodity prices and can reduce operating margins or market share by making one company's product more competitive than another's.

That is where this book fits in. While a vast field of literature in both the technical aspects of foreign exchange management and financial engineering fills the shelves of many corporate libraries, and while a rich bank of writings on strategic management and competitive advantage also exists, the approach of this book is new in that we view financial engineering as a tactical skill which can produce strong leverage if looked upon and managed from a strategic perspective.

Part one of this book offers a five-step approach to developing a strategic risk management program. Part two, on the other hand, shares the insights of five multinational corporations that are successfully managing either transactional and economic financial risks, or both. It explores how they developed their hedging programs, and how such programs have impacted company performance.

The risk management stakes for many corporations are steep—as the plight of the U.S. auto industry in the last decade has shown. It's a personal belief of ours that price volatility (and corporate treasury's ability to manage it) has already impacted many competitors within many global industry sectors and will continue to significantly impact the financial performance and market shares of many more corporations worldwide. The bottom line: Superior technology, cheap labor, and superior distribution no longer ensure a company's success;

depending on its operational make-up, balance sheet, and raw material inputs and outputs, it must also pay attention to fluctuating prices in exchange rates, interest rates, and commodity prices. Whether corporate officers admit it or not, all of these variables can often impact widget makers just as much as the quality of their widgets. The central issue is that increasing rates of price volatility directly impact any firm's price/quality ratio and therefore its competitive advantage.

It is out hope that this book gives testimony to the wisdom and sophistication many corporations have in managing exposures to price volatility, while at the same time offering a strategic framework for other corporations and their officers who want to respond proactively to a more globally competitive and volatile economic environment.

MARK J. AHN
WILLIAM D. FALLOON

Exhibit 1

Mentor Graphics Corporation
8500 S.W. Creekside Place
Beaverton, OR 97005-7191
(503) 626-7000
Telex: 160577MENTOR UT

March 1, 1990

Mr. Edmund Coulson
Chief Accountant
Room 4917 Mail Stop 4-8
Office of the Chief Accountant
Securities Exchange Commission
450 Fifth Street Northwest
Washington, D.C. 20549

Dear Mr. Coulson:

We have read the SEC's statements (made at the June 29, 1989 meeting of the Emerging Issues Task Force) regarding hedges of net income. It is our studied opinion that, for reasons enumerated below, the accounting treatment currently recommended will prevent companies from undertaking activities that are optimal from an economic standpoint.

The SEC observer at the June 29 meeting stated that, *"...a foreign subsidiary's future revenues or costs denominated in that subsidiary's functional currency do not expose either the subsidiary or the parent to foreign currency risk capable of being hedged for accounting purposes"*.

To demonstrate an alternative view, assume the following:

- Earnings volatility is a reasonable proxy for a US dollar corporation's risk.
- The corporation has a major non-US dollar subsidiary.

As the subsidiary's earnings stream (constant from period to period in functional currency units) is translated back to dollars, exchange rate fluctuations become embodied in the consolidated US dollar net income. As a result, the comparative earnings numbers are subject to extreme volatility solely as a result of FX fluctuations (see attached example). The adverse effect of this translation volatility on Mentor Graphics' consolidated international revenue will be in excess of $6 million in 1989 (on a base of $200 million). This equates to a five percent swing in consolidated EPS. This risk could be, in large part, mitigated by using currency options to hedge a forecasted net income stream. This short example is demonstrative of a real exposure, capable of being hedged for accounting purposes.

The SEC observer has also stated that, *"...hedge accounting requires identifying specific transactions, assets, or liabilities ...and therefore hedging net income is inappropriate"*.

Exhibit 1 (continued)

Mr. Edmund Coulson
March 1, 1990
Page Two

The accounting profession needs to identify the true economic substance of transactions and allow the accounting pronouncements to properly and conservatively reflect this substance. Mentor Graphics Corporation has deemed that hedging net income is appropriate if the company elects to reduce FX volatility in sequential earning periods. We have identified options as the most appropriate vehicle to use for this purpose.

In order to properly reflect the economic substance of net income hedging, options used for this purpose must qualify for hedge accounting (with gains deferred until exposure losses materialize) or, if the SEC maintains that these options are speculative in nature, then a mark to market requirement must not be imposed. The mark to market requirement produces results contrary to the objectives of the SEC and the FASB: Earnings are obfuscated by the inclusion of gains which are not earnings; and volatility is induced in the income statement.

Support for suggestions espoused here is prevalent throughout current trade journals. In addition, the accounting treatment I recommend is not without precedent in GAAP:

- Not recognizing unrealized gains in the income statement is conservative accounting treatment.

- FASB 80 paragraph 9 allows hedge treatment for transaction, "an enterprise expects, ...in the normal course of business".

- Marketable equity securities and inventory both follow the lower of cost of market concept which does not allow gains to be recognized in the financial statements until realized.

- FASB 5 paragraph 17 states, "Contingencies that might result in gains usually are not reflected in the accounts since to do so might be to recognize revenue prior to its realization". The contingency with respect to an FX option is the ultimate exercise or sale of that instrument; an event which may or may not occur.

In summary, I urge the SEC to alter its position on this issue by recognizing net income hedges as legitimate and by allowing options used for such a purpose to qualify for hedge accounting. Thank you for considering our views on this matter.

Sincerely,

MENTOR GRAPHICS CORPORATION

Brian C. Henry
Vice President and Chief Financial Officer

cc: Joseph F. Hoffman, Peat Marwick Main & Co. .
    Tim Lucas, FASB

Exhibit 1 (continued)

EXAMPLE - TRANSLATION EXPOSURE

	PERIOD 1 & 2 YEN	PERIOD 1 US$ (123 YEN/US$)	PERIOD 2 US$ (133 YEN/US$)
Revenue	1,000,000,000	$8,130,081	$7,518,797
Cost of Sales	400,000,000	$3,252,033	$3,007,519
Gross Margin	600,000,000	$4,878,049	$4,511,278
Operating Expenses	450,000,000	$3,658,537	$3,383,459
Operating Margin	150,000,000	$1,219,512	$1,127,820
Other Income/Expense	5,000,000	$40,650	$37,594
Income Taxes	93,000,000	$756,098	$699,248
Net Income	52,000,000	$422,764	$390,977

- Hypothetical performance of wholly owned Japanese subsidiary
- Yen performance is identical in periods 1 & 2
- Exchange rates moved from 123 Yen/US$ in period 1 to 133 Yen/US$ in period 2 (Equivalent to Q1 & Q2 1989)
- Consolidated US$ P&L volatility greatly exacerbated by FX rate fluctuations

Exhibit 2

SYNTEX CORPORATION
3401 HILLVIEW AVENUE, P.O. BOX 10850
PALO ALTO, CALIFORNIA 94303

(415) 855-5050
TELEX 4997273 SYNTEX PLA

November 2, 1990

Mr. Joseph Erickson
Financial Accounting Standards Board
401 Merritt 7
Norwalk, Connecticut 06856

Dear Joseph,

It was a pleasure speaking with you on Wednesday, in regards to the currency hedge accounting issues facing the accounting profession. As promised, I have enclosed a letter outlining our views and concerns relating to hedge accounting.

Thank you for this opportunity to provide input to a most important task.

Sincerely,

Stephen Y. Fong
Manager, International Treasury

cc: Alan Stevenson
    Hans Schmid

PIT/1425

Exhibit 2 (continued)

SYNTEX CORPORATION
3401 HILLVIEW AVENUE, P.O. BOX 10850
PALO ALTO, CALIFORNIA 94303

(415) 855-5050
TELEX 4997273 SYNTEX PLA

November 2, 1990

Mr. Joseph Erickson
Financial Accounting Standards Board
401 Merritt 7
Norwalk, Connecticut 06856

Dear Joseph,

Recently, we received a copy of issues summary 90-17 on "Hedging Foreign Currency Risks With Purchased Options". The summary was very comprehensive and does an excellent job in addressing the many complex issues surrounding hedging activities. We have analyzed this summary and accordingly wish to provide input to the FASB for consideration.

The issues addressed are very complex and in some cases controversial. But most importantly, these issues have great impact on the ongoing ability of U.S. businesses to compete in world markets. Accordingly, my first point is that any decisions should be made after careful consideration and due process. Although I would like to see specific guidance materialize in the near future, such guidance should not be at the expense of due process, which allows for careful consideration of numerous views.

Any decision on hedge accounting can significantly impact the competitiveness of American industry at large. For years U.S. based businesses suffered from an overvalued dollar. Many American industries watched helplessly as the strong dollar eroded both their market share and profitability. Today, American industry is once again price competitive in the international arena, thanks to a weak dollar. Many companies are interested in protecting this competitive advantage via hedging. However, since many of these companies are publicly held, accounting and reported results are of significant consequence. In fact, an overwhelming majority would forgo protecting this competitiveness if faced with adverse accounting implications. This is a situation where accounting can severely hamper good sound business decisions. We believe that accounting should properly reflect the results of business decisions, rather than drive them. Because of its pervasive impact, these decisions should not be made in haste. We urge the FASB to carefully consider industry views before any decision is made.

With respect to various points addressed in the issues summary, we offer the following points for consideration.

Exhibit 2 (continued)

First, the focus should be shifted away from specific hedging instruments. A focus on specific hedging instruments will undoubtedly fail as new instruments are constantly being developed. Rather, a shift in focus to the basics of hedging may prove more useful. The FASB board should focus on the substance of hedging as opposed to the form. We believe hedge accounting treatment should be afforded to any hedging instrument that is effective in reducing risk associated with an underlying economic exposure. To clarify this statement, some definitions are in order.

The first term that must be defined is "hedging". Most of us in industry would define hedging as an act taken to reduce the enterprise's risks to adverse price changes. Prices in this context include interest rates, the price of inputs (raw material, energy, etc.), outputs, and exchange rates. The focus of hedging is to avoid adverse price impacts. We focus on the term adverse because most enterprises are not interested in avoiding favorable price impacts.

Next, hedge accounting must be defined. Hedge accounting should allow for the deferral of any gains, losses, or costs associated with the hedging instrument, for later measurement with the underlying hedged exposure. For example, if a company wishes to hedge anticipated exports to Germany, the treasurer may purchase a DM put option for $100,000. Hedge accounting should allow the company to defer the $100,000 cost and any interim gains on the option until the anticipated export is realized. At the time of realization, the cost and any gain on the option should be booked to sales along with the actual export sale.

Another term that requires definition is economic exposure. We propose to use the FASB52 definition of exposures with minor modifications. We would extend the FASB52 definition to include anticipated transactions as defined in FASB80. We believe that exposures often exist long before a shipment takes place. Many of these exposures represent ongoing business with familiar customers. However, in most cases, there are no binding contracts to ensure ongoing business. Hence, no firm committments. In laymans terms, we would define economic exposures as a risk of adverse changes in the enterprise's cash flows that may result from price (exchange rate) changes.

Lastly, we would like to define risk reduction. We believe that risk reduction can take many forms. An enterprise can reduce its risk by: 1) changing the underlying exposure (i.e., changing the currency denomination of the transaction); 2) entering into a contract to transfer the exposure to a third party (in substance, this is what is done when companies enter into forward exchange contracts); 3) entering into a contract with a third party to transfer any adverse impacts resulting from a price change. (This is commonly done through purchases of options). All of the above actions serve to reduce enterprise risk by transferring in cases 1) and 2), the entire exposure, or in case 3) just the adverse component of exposures.

Exhibit 2 (continued)

To summarize, we believe that any hedging instruments which serve to reduce enterprise risk should qualify for hedge accounting treatment as previously defined. This is consistent with paragraph 42 in FASB80. However we would modify FASB80's definition of risk reduction to include the concept of reducing risk to adverse affects of price changes.

Subissue 3 on page 15 of the issues summary deals with this concept. Again, we urge the Board to focus on the substance of risk reduction. Risk reduction need not be limited to two sided neutralization of gains and losses. When we think of risk, we always think of risk to adversity. The term risk is inconsistent with a favorable outcome. Any correlation questions should be applied to the adverse component of the hedged exposures. Hedging does not necessarily have to neutralize gains as well as losses in order to be effective.

While on the subject of FASB80, we applaud the recognition that anticipated transactions represent enterprise risk even though no firm commitment exists. We believe that FASB52 is far too restrictive in requiring firm commitments to allow for hedge accounting treatment. Virtually 100% of our export business takes place without any prior firm commitments! This concept of firm commitment may fit certain industries where long manufacturing lead times are required, but for the rest of us, it is not applicable.

Earlier we stressed the need for careful consideration of all views before a decision is made. At the same time we understand the need to address numerous inconsistencies currently in existence. If the EITF feels compelled to make any decision on November 8, 1990, we strongly urge the following solution:

Expand FASB80 to include all forms of price risk (including currency). Expand the financial instruments covered under FASB80 to include options.

We believe that "substance over form" objectives support the above modifications. From the standpoint of price risk, the risk associated with the price of deutsche marks is no different from the risk associated with the price of oil. It seems rather silly that an oil company can hedge its uncommitted future sales of oil while a pharmaceutical company can't hedge it's uncommitted future sales of life enhancing medications. Both companies are exposed to price risk associated with the future sales of its products. Both companies should be free to protect those sales and receive similar accounting treatment. The form of these risks differ, but in substance, they are the same. They both represent price risk. FASB80 limits hedge accounting to very specific hedging instruments. Again, we believe that substance over form should prevail. There is no logical reason to limit hedging instruments to exchange traded futures contracts. We feel the focus should be on the risk reduction characteristics of the hedging instrument as a basis for determining applicability under FASB80. To reiterate, we believe that any financial instrument that is effective in reducing enterprise risk should be afforded hedge accounting treatment.

Exhibit 2 (continued)

In summary, we believe that the FASB is in a unique position to either benefit or hurt U.S. industry, depending on its' decisions regarding hedge accounting. An adverse decision on hedge accounting will significantly hamper U.S. industry's ability to manage basic business risks. We strongly urge the Board to allow hedge accounting for all instruments or actions, that are effective in reducing enterprise risk. Fundamentally, if a hedge instrument is effective as a hedge, that instrument should receive hedge accounting treatment.

Thank you for this opportunity to provide input to a very important function. Please feel free to contact me with any questions you may have.

Sincerely,

Stephen Y. Fong
Manager, International Treasury

cc: Alan Stevenson
      Hans Schmid

PART ONE

Understanding Strategic Risk Management

1

Introduction: Managing Financial Risk in the 1990s

"Perception is strong and sight is weak."

—MIYAMOTO MUSASHI, *A BOOK OF FIVE RINGS*

"As you begin to move from the accounting definition of exposure, you lose your security blanket. The accounting definition is very precise, but it is not accurate. The question that accuracy asks is, what is the real problem?"

—DAVID FIEDLER,
Director of Foreign Exchange Planning,
Eastman Kodak

Since the advent of floating exchange rates in 1973, an era of violent turbulence has characterized international financial markets. As a corollary, the impact of seemingly ever-increasing foreign exchange rate gyrations on the multinational firm's competitive position is being felt in boardrooms worldwide. Moreover, the financial impact of market turbulence on cash flows and firm valuation is causing a sea of change in the way in which both financial and general managers think, organize and execute exposure management programs in transnational corporations.

3

In the past, the Statement of Financial Accounting Standards Board No. 52 fit the needs of the accounting and treasury department constituencies very well. The major features of FASB 52 are (1) income statement items must be recorded at the actual or weighted rate at the time of recognition and (2) translation adjustments bypass the income statement and are accumulated in a separate section called cumulative translation adjustment. This enabled CEOs and CFOs to avoid the wild variations in net income caused by presumably non-cash flow items in the balance sheet.

The treasury department was likewise happy because hedging rules and exposures were defined. Only narrowly defined, individually identified payables and receivables were hedged. In short, the treasurer's world was known (or defined)—and so were his responsibilities.

The accounting department was happy because the universe of exposure was laid out by the Financial Accounting Standards Board (FASB). Unfortunately, FASB so narrowly defined the exposure which qualified for hedge accounting that no one saw the freight train of economic exposure barreling straight into going concerns.

And a funny thing happened on the way to globalization.

In 1973, the U.S. exported only 5 percent or $71 billion of GNP in goods and services. By 1989, the U.S. exported $362 billion in goods and services. Moreover, since 1973—through recessions, depressions, oil shocks, and stagflation—multilateral trade continues to increase at a rate faster than world production. In fact, from 1980 to 1988, world output grew 26 percent; and during the same period, world trade grew 37 percent.

In March 1973, the U.S. dollar was permanently allowed to float. The floating exchange rate era has coincided with an unprecedented growth in cross-border investment flows, trade growth and economic opportunity. According to the Geneva-based trade agency GATT, the value of goods traded globally in 1989 rose 7.5 percent to reach $3.1 trillion. Moreover, manufactured goods accounted for over 80 percent of the 1989 increase. Only 5 years ago, by comparison, global trade was less than $2 trillion.

Further, competition among nations for an increasing portion of the global export pie has been a major impetus for product and management innovation (See Figure 1.1). Perhaps more importantly, however, the dynamism of the post-World War II export environment has induced dramatic structural changes in production and distribution systems. After dominating the world export market during the 1950s and 1960s, Japan and Germany have equaled the U.S. in their share of global exports in absolute terms. Japan, Germany and the U.S. collectively have 34 percent or $977 billion of total world exports of $2,892 billion.

The convergence of export market shares has necessarily increased the vulnerability and price sensitivity of international trade. Thus, while the pie of international trade has certainly expanded in absolute terms, so has the risk of price and market share erosion due to factors such as currency fluctuations.

Figure 1.1   World Export and Trade Shares (1960–1988)

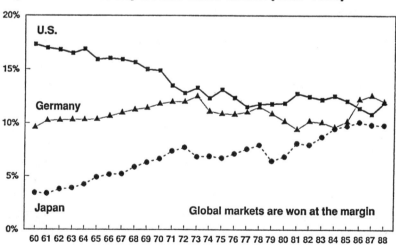

5

Year-on-Year Percentage Change
(March 1973–March 1990)

	DEM/USD	JPY/USD	GBP/USD	CAD/USD
AVERAGE	-1.6%	-2.4%	-1.6%	1.0%
MINIMUM	-29.1%	-35.6%	-25.8%	-8.6%
MAXIMUM	38.3%	29.7%	31.2%	10.4%
STANDARD DEVIATION	12.4%	12.4%	11.8%	4.3%

During the floating rate period between March 1973 to March 1990, wide fluctuations from parity measures have been the norm, often wiping out or helping productivity and efficiency gains resulting from capital investment. During this period, the Deutsche mark changed up to 38 percent in a 12-month period versus the U.S. dollar; and the Japanese yen changed up to 35.6 percent (See Figures 1.2 and 1.3).

The effects of such foreign exchange volatility can wreak havoc on expensive and hard-fought productivity gains. Caterpillar, for example, began a $2 billion capital investment program called *Plant With A Future* (PWAF) beginning in 1987. The Illinois-based program successfully decreased the incidence of faulty transmissions from 4 to 2 percent, with a full cost reduction of 19 percent eventually expected in 1993. During the same period, however, the Japanese yen weakened against the U.S. dollar by 30 percent which placed Caterpillar at a competitive disadvantage vis-à-vis its major competitor, Komatsu of Japan— even after adjusting for productivity gains! In fact, the reward of streamlining operations may simply be survival for the American heavy equipment firm who stated in the *Wall Street Journal* that it "may not be able to raise prices at all this year (1990)—and may even have to offer discounts" to clear inventory.

The result of rapid international trade growth and increased financial volatility has thus permanently redefined the market structures faced by firms. In order to cope with increasing uncertainty, the structure of transnationals began changing from insular multi-domestic industries to global organizations relying upon often

6

Figure 1.2   Japanese Yen / U.S. Dollar: Year-on-Year Percent Change (March 1973–March 1990)

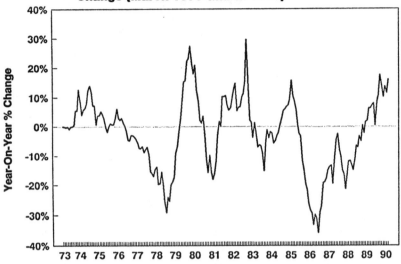

Figure 1.3   Deutsche Mark / U.S. Dollar: Year-on-Year Percent Change (March 1973–March 1990)

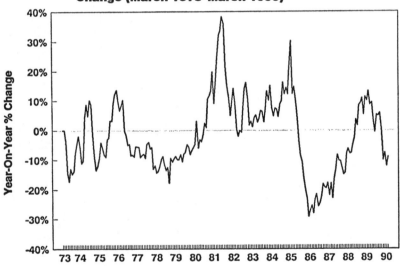

Figure 1.4   The Imperative for Proactive Financial Risk Management Increases with Volatility and Globalization

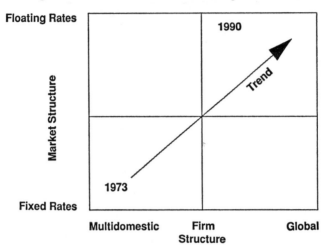

ill-defined matrix charts to lead the way. Multifunctional coordination has replaced functional expertise almost overnight as firms attempt to empower teams of employees to gain and maintain competitive advantage (See Figure 1.4).

While financial markets are truly global in scope, multinational treasury departments have not generally linked the technical "financial engineering" aspects of risk management with strategic planning on the firm level. In other words, the treasury department is still relying on functional expertise in a global environment. In practical terms, the ability to calculate an option premium or forward points is not the same as managing the impact of currency fluctuations on the firm's competitive position. The playing field and goals have suddenly become uneven and murky, leaving the treasury department searching for answers. The new imperative is for the financial risk manager to recognize the impact of currency and interest rate fluctuations on firm value—and take responsibility for the impacts on valuation and competitive position.

As the following examples illustrate, this challenge can have dramatic effects on firm valuation and competitive advantage.

- In 1986, Sony of Japan reported a number of pathbreaking products and new market entry accomplishments. Despite increased volume, Sony was pummeled by the strengthening yen which caused a decline in sales of 7 percent, in operating income of 75 percent and net income of 43 percent.

- Eastman Kodak's 1988 annual report stated "the effects of worldwide currency changes against the U.S. dollar added approximately $250 million to 1988 sales."

  Then, on Wednesday, May 3, 1989, *The Wall Street Journal* ran an article that mapped out the battlefield. The article on Kodak was ominously entitled "…1st Period Net Plunged 23 percent; Exchange Rates Blamed, Stock Slides." The article went on to report that "Kodak's cash cows—film, with flat revenue, and photographic paper, which had an estimated 7 percent revenue drop—have been hurt by pricing. Unfavorable currency exchange rates have left the company with higher costs overseas, but unable to raise prices because of stiff competition."

- The foreign exchange skies were quite unfriendly to United Airlines who reported foreign exchange transaction losses of $41.2 million in 1988. In fact, over the last 3 years UAL has lost $107.7 million in currency transaction losses.

- Pan Am Corporation experienced a consolidated net loss of $72.7 million in 1988—of which $36.4 million or 50 percent were foreign exchange transaction losses.

- During 1986 through 1988, Texas Air Corporation nearly doubled revenues from $4.4 billion to $8.6 billion riding the wave of Frank

Lorenzo's buying spree of Continental Airlines, Eastern Airlines and People's Express. During the 3-year period, Texas Air had a cumulative operating income of $128.6 million. Over the same period, Texas Air lost $37.5 million in foreign exchange transactional exposure.

- Zenith Electronic Corp's second quarter 1989 loss of $13 million was "caused principally by currency value shifts, increased interest expense, and lower margins on computer sales." The company's Chairman and President, Jerry K. Pearlman, said in a *Wall Street Journal* "our currency positioning, which didn't permit us to operate at prevailing currency market rates, resulted in a lost profit opportunity of about $5 million in the second quarter. And, if exchange rates remain where they are today, the second half effect could be about $20 million."

- On February 21, 1990, the *Financial Times* reported that the venerable Honda Motor of Japan posted reported a drop of 7.8 percent in consolidated quarterly earnings "mainly because of a large foreign exchange loss."

- On February 28, 1990, the *Financial Times* reported annual profits for Unilever, the Dutch-Anglo food and consumer products group, increased 24 percent to GBP 1.8 billion in 1989. The company also announced that if the British pound had not weakened during the year, profits would have increased only 13 percent. Thus, currency fluctuations accounted for 46 percent of Unilever's annual profit.

- On April 4, 1990, the *Financial Times* reported "Hoechst earnings suffer due to strong D-mark." The German chemical group saw pre-tax earnings drop 10 percent and reported that without foreign exchange losses "full year earnings would have been DEM 100 million (U.S. dollar 59 million) higher...[which would have] translated into a 4 percent rise in 1989 pre-tax profit."

10

The point of highlighting these articles is that currency fluctuations (1) impact shareholder value, (2) force trade-offs between market share and profit margins, and (3) impact the firm's cost of capital. And the point of this book is that while currency hedging is not a panacea for product quality, it is an integral component of the value chain which should be proactively managed.

Foreign exchange management for the 1990s is about managing change and multifunctional coordination. In Peter Drucker's *The New Realities*, he notes that managers must "...accept responsibility for protecting the business against foreign exchange risks just as they are responsible for protecting the business against any other foreseeable risk."

Forces Driving Strategic Hedging

Managing strategically requires the recognition of enabling and threatening forces affecting the planning process. To be sure, shaping these forces, especially macroeconomic forces, is normally out of the firm's direct control. However, a flexible response to these underlying drivers will determine whether a firm is a proactive market leader or a reactive follower in today's global economy.

Macroeconomic Drivers

The pace of globalization has induced dramatic macroeconomic shifts in transaction costs, interdependence, and competitive threats. This section will review major macroeconomic drivers shaping foreign exchange management alternatives.

In his seminal work, *The Case for Flexible Exchange Rates* in 1953, Milton Freidman stated "...a system of flexible or floating exchange rates—exchange rates freely determined in an open market primarily by private dealings and, like other market prices, varying from day-to-day—[are] absolutely essential for the fulfillment of our basic economic objective—the achievement and maintenance of a free and prosperous world community engaging in unrestricted multilateral trade."

Since the floating currency period began in March 1973, the floating exchange rate regime has been credited and maligned with many characteristics. Not the least of these characteristics are increased rates of volatility which have led nominal exchange rates far away from Purchasing Power Parity (PPP) and Interest Rate Parity (IRP) measures. PPP measures the deviation of exchange rates from inflation differentials over time. IRP, on the other hand attempts to explain real currency over- or under-valuations by interest rate differentials. This development has been underscored by a decoupling of the capital market from the goods and services market. This decoupling poses a tremendous risk to multinational firms because foreign exchange rates are driven by what the Argentines call "capital golondrina"— that is, "hot money", which flows as fast and fluidly as the swallows fly from Buenos Aires to Capistrano, dominates foreign exchange markets.

A New York Federal Reserve Bank census found that over 95 percent of all currency volume is traded between financial firms such as money center banks like Union Bank of Switzerland, Citibank and Chase Manhattan Bank. In fact, only 4.9 percent of foreign exchange volume is attributable to transactions related to goods and services! Further, latest estimates place daily currency trading volume at over $500 billion. A separate study estimated currency trading volume at 32 times world trade.

Increased volatility and volume has also transformed the function of currency from primarily a medium of exchange to a true commodity—complete with liquid markets and derivative products. Of course, the corollary to increased volatility is increased risk.

As can be seen in the following table and graphs, actual rates have deviated from parity rates by as much as 72 percent in the case of the Deutsche mark versus the U.S. dollar; and 49 percent in the case of the Japanese yen versus the U.S. dollar (See Table 1.1 and Figures 1.5 through 1.12).

Table 1.1 Foreign Exchange Rate Statistics (March 1973–March 1990)

	DEM/USD	JPY/USD	GBP/USD	CAD/USD
AVERAGE	2.26	224.24	$1.84	1.18
MINIMUM	1.57	121.05	$1.07	0.96
MAXIMUM	3.36	305.15	$2.58	1.42
STANDARD DEVIATION	0.39	54.24	$0.35	0.13

	PPP DEM/USD	PPP JPY/USD	PPP GBP/USD	PPP CAD/USD
AVERAGE	2.21	276.64	$1.67	1.07
MINIMUM	1.74	221.92	$1.35	1.00
MAXIMUM	2.85	334.35	$2.48	1.15
STANDARD DEVIATION	0.36	34.84	$0.32	0.05

	IRP DEM/USD	IRP JPY/USD	IRP GBP/USD	IRP CAD/USD
AVERAGE	2.73	250.75	$1.75	1.15
MINIMUM	2.22	188.41	$1.52	1.00
MAXIMUM	3.08	287.04	$2.48	1.29
STANDARD DEVIATION	0.29	31.76	$0.27	0.08

	PPP % CHG FROM DEM/USD	PPP % CHG FROM JPY/USD	PPP % CHG FROM GBP/USD	PPP % CHG FROM CAD/USD
AVERAGE	-4.1%	19.5%	10.8%	-9.5%
MINIMUM	-71.8%	-6.7%	-27.1%	-27.6%
MAXIMUM	25.0%	48.8%	55.2%	6.5%
STANDARD DEVIATION	21.2%	15.2%	16.5%	8.7%

	IRP % CHG FROM DEM/USD	IRP % CHG FROM JPY/USD	IRP % CHG FROM GBP/USD	IRP % CHG FROM CAD/USD
AVERAGE	16.5%	11.5%	$1.84	-2.1%
MINIMUM	-33.5%	-13.1%	$1.07	-16.9%
MAXIMUM	41.6%	41.1%	$2.58	9.6%
STANDARD DEVIATION	15.0%	15.0%	$0.35	6.1%

Figure 1.5   Deutsche Mark / U.S. Dollar
(March 1973–March 1990)

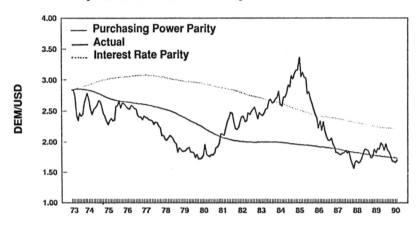

Figure 1.6   Deutsche Mark / U.S. Dollar: Over (Under) Valuation
Percent from Parity
(March 1973–March 1990)

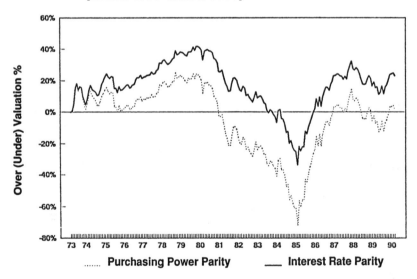

**Figure 1.7   Japanese Yen / U.S. Dollar
(March 1973–March 1990)**

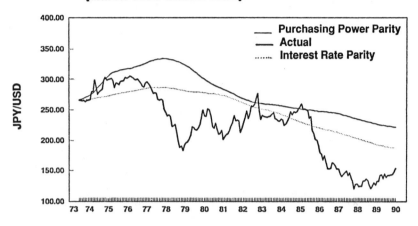

**Figure 1.8   Japanese Yen / U.S. Dollar: Over (Under) Valuation
Percent from Parity
(March 1973–March 1990)**

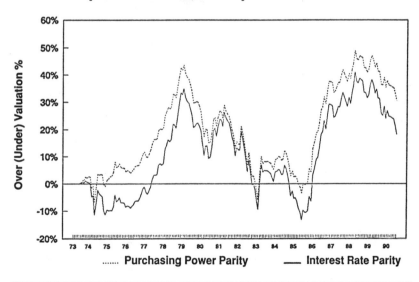

Figure 1.9   British Pound / U.S. Dollar
(March 1973–March 1990)

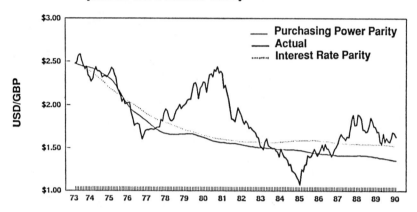

Figure 1.10 British Pound / U.S. Dollar: Over (Under) Valuation
Percent from Parity
(March 1973–March 1990)

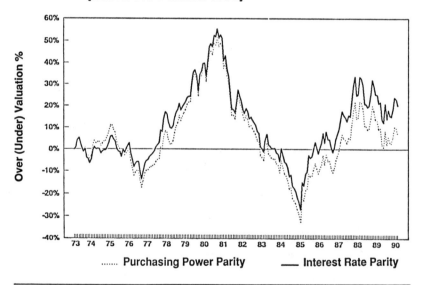

**Figure 1.11 Canadian Dollar / U.S. Dollar
(March 1973–March 1990)**

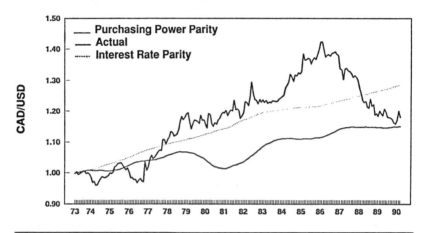

**Figure 1.12 Canadian Dollar / U.S. Dollar: Over (Under) Valuation
Percent from Parity
(March 1973–March 1990)**

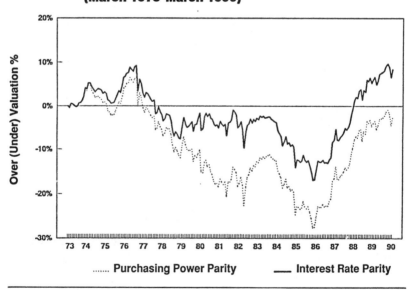

Economists generally agree that large deviations from parity are driven by the speed differences between currency markets to assimilate information into exchange rates and the goods market to adjust prices. As the Scottish economist R. MacDonald concluded, "the asymmetrical nature of adjustment speeds in goods and asset markets...is one explanation for the failure of PPP to hold. PPP may also have failed to hold in the recent past because of structural changes in the world economy which required real exchange rate changes. For example, during the 1970s the United States was less efficient in the production of tradeables than its competitors, such as Japan and West Germany, and this required bilateral real exchange rate changes. The discovery and production of oil in the UK in the 1970s necessitated a real exchange rate change."

What does wide and prolonged deviations from parity measures mean for general and financial managers? Simply put, profit margins and market share are always at stake. Considering that average U.S. corporate profits during 1973 - 1989 were 5.1 percent, firms stand to sustain tremendous risk from wide parity deviations. Even firms which have totally domestic sales and costs are exposed. For example, a strengthening of the U.S. dollar in the early 1980s invited many foreign market entrants to aggressively price in U.S. dollar terms and take market share — without giving up margins in their home currency.

Perhaps the most reported example during the 1980s was the decline of the U.S. auto industry at the hands of Japanese and to a lesser extent German manufacturers. The meteoric rise in the U.S. dollar opened up an opportunity to aggressively seize market share and still produce margins to maintain strong capital investment programs. When the U.S. dollar began its decline in March 1985, Japanese producers established an American manufacturing presence to counter declining yen revenues. The result? Japanese auto manufacturers have increased their U.S. market share every year during the 1980s.

In fact, a study by G.H. Anderson and J.B. Carlson of the Federal Reserve found that the successful navigation of Japanese automakers in the U.S. during the 1980s was a result of:

(1) An extensive use of hedging to manage medium-term flows which were especially critical when the yen strengthened by 85.1 percent in U.S. dollar terms from March 1985 to December 1987.

(2) A shift of cost structure from Japan to Korea and other low-cost newly industrialized countries, as well as transplant facilities in the U.S..

(3) Voluntary Export Restraints (VER) forced by the U.S. Congress, which limit the number of Japanese cars that may be imported into the U.S.. The VER has actually increased the retail price of autos by approximately $1,114, even after adjusting for inflation and quality changes.

On an international level, the current account is the broadest scorecard or measure of a country's ability to win in the global marketplace. The current account is the sum of a country's merchandise trade balance plus net financial transfers. During the floating rate period between 1973 to 1989, the current account surpluses of Japan and Germany have roughly equaled the deficits of the United States (See Figure 1.13). The U.S. is losing, but the race is far from over. Past success means nothing in the 1990s, with product technologies such as superconductivity and lasers threatening to routinely cannibalize whole markets as a matter of course. The firms and nations that win in the 1990s will be characterized as learning organizations that embrace change and offer flexible responses to customer requirements. When the yen began to strengthen in the mid-1980s, for example, Sony initiated a downsizing program for the Walkman product line to decrease costs by miniaturizing and combining components. Since the Walkman was first introduced in 1980, 170 new models have been released and the number of components have been reduced by a third.

Since stock valuation impacts a firm's cost of capital and competitive advantage, another way of viewing the impact of volatility on a

**Figure 1.13 Current Account: U.S., Japan & Germany
(1973–1989)**

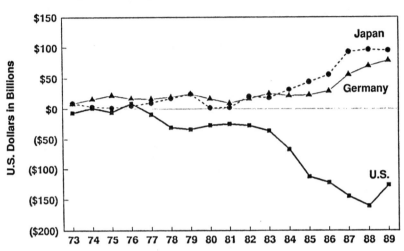

company is the effect of currency changes on international equity values. During the floating rate period between March 1973 and March 1990, the U.S. stock market has not rewarded investors with a return commensurate with prevailing risk. For example, an American investor with a portfolio replicating the Dow Jones Industrial Average (DJIA) would have earned an annual return of 7.7 percent with a standard deviation of 17.6 percent. However, a Japanese yen-based investor would have earned an average return of 5.0 percent with a standard deviation of 19.1 percent. In comparison, an American investor with a portfolio replicating the Nikkei index would have earned an annual average U.S. dollar return of 12.9 percent with a standard deviation of 18.9 percent. This means that for 7 percent more risk during the March 1973 to March 1990 period, a U.S. dollar-based investor would have earned 68 percent more return in the Tokyo stock market! (See Table 1.2 and Figure 1.14).

Table1.2   Year-on-Year Percent Equity Market Returns (March 1973–March 1989)

	USD-BASED INVESTOR	JPY-BASED INVESTOR	DEM-BASED INVESTOR
1. United States Stock Market			
AVERAGE	7.7%	5.0%	3.8%
MINIMUM	-32.6%	-38.2%	-52.1%
MAXIMUM	50.8%	45.8%	60.5%
STANDARD DEVIATION	17.6%	19.1%	25.7%
2. German Stock Market			
AVERAGE	7.9%	2.8%	5.0%
MINIMUM	-38.8%	-55.8%	-52.4%
MAXIMUM	82.3%	49.8%	41.3%
STANDARD DEVIATION	21.8%	19.6%	17.3%
3. Japan Stock Market			
AVERAGE	12.9%	10.3%	12.5%
MINIMUM	-35.2%	-22.8%	-35.3%
MAXIMUM	64.8%	33.0%	52.0%
STANDARD DEVIATION	18.9%	10.0%	17.4%

Equity Markets Values Are Converging

Another measure of capital market equalization is the convergence of equity capitalization among the world's largest trading nations. For example, the U.S., Japan and Western Europe share a nearly equal portion of world stock market capitalization (see Table 1.3).

Not only have world equity markets converged in value, international holdings have also been globalized. In fact, cross-border equity holdings were estimated to total over $600 billion at the end of 1989.

21

**Figure 1.14 Equity Markets: U.S., Japan & Germany
(March 1973–March 1990)**

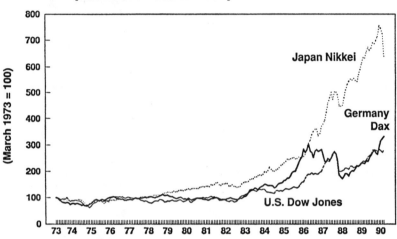

Table 1.3   1990 World Stock Market Capitalization

	USD Billions	Percent of Total
World	$8,706.0	100.0%
U.S.	$3,055.8	35.1%
Japan	$2,751.0	31.6%
Europe	$2,394.2	27.5%

The Role of the U.S. Dollar Is Declining

A further factor influencing the imperative of proactive risk management is the diminishing role of the U.S. dollar. During the past 5 years, the dollar's share of cross border lending contracted from 72 to 53 percent. Other factors eroding the dollar-standard include: (1) financial deregulation, which has increased the scope for the international use of certain currencies, (2) the growing importance of non-U.S. banks, (3) lower interest rates in currencies like the Japanese yen and

22

Deutsche mark which have boosted demand in non-dollar borrowings, (4) the growth of Pacific Rim countries, where the yen plays a dominant role, and (5) rescheduling and debt reduction programs that have resulted in some non-U.S. banks switching third world loans from dollar to domestic currencies.

Leverage Has Decreased America's Competitive Position

In the global arena of high currency market volatility, the sensitivity of the business environment to foreign exchange rate fluctuations has also increased with the popularity of leverage. In 1950, interest expense took 15 cents of each gross profit dollar; it now takes over 70 cents in cash flow (earnings plus depreciation) terms. Moreover, 56 percent of cash flow has gone to interest expense during the 1980s—as compared to 16 percent in the 1960s and 33 percent in the 1970s.

Operating leverage has also been exacerbated by a decrease in corporate America's net worth. The net worth of American businesses has fallen from 95 percent of GNP in 1980 to 74 percent of GNP in 1988.

Not to be outdone by corporations, the U.S. government is the first major debtor nation in history to owe all of its debt in its own currency. The phenomena of public and private sector leverage has not only mortgaged America's future and decapitalized the nation's equity base, but has also hamstrung the Federal Reserve's ability to respond to a financial crisis. The Fed has two functions—(1) to restrict money supply growth and (2) act as the lender of last resort. The economy's precarious debt load could send the Fed to the printing press in the event of a recession. At best, this would mean a period of inflation. At worst, a monetization would induce a vicious cycle of late 1970s style stagflation—inflation and low growth. Either outcome would require managers to remain nimble in order to survive a period of severe financial turbulence

23

Exports Are Redefining the Economic Map

Another driving force is the role of exports in reshaping the global economic map. The floating exchange rate regime has also witnessed an explosion of international trade. In 1959, the U.S. exported 0.4 percent of GNP; and in 1989, the U.S. exported only 5.9 percent of GNP. Comparatively, in 1989, Germany exported 39 percent of GNP; and Japan exported 14.5 percent of GNP. The composition of trade imbalances also raises the spectre of protectionism from myopic politicians and uncompetitive industrial sectors.

"Global Regionalism" Is Making the Nation State Obsolete

Regional blocs are having an increasing influence on the terms of trade, investment and currency flows. The diminishing need for defense spending is creating a seamless demographic structure whereby the base country of a corporation is becoming increasingly irrelevant. U.S. policy makers, for example, are waging a battle with Europeans on behalf of Honda and other Japanese auto makers to export American-made cars to the European Economic Community (EEC).

Further, the declining importance of natural resources is compounding the preeminence of human resources. Nations are no longer competing with ideologies, but rather results as measured by quality of life and standards of living. The declining importance of military spending and natural resources will have important consequences for investment flows and capital markets. An example of global resource development is Otis Elevator's objective of developing a customized Elevonic 411 at the lowest possible cost. The United Technologies Corporation subsidiary developed the new elevator in six research centers across five countries simultaneously. The U.S. group handled the systems integration, a Japanese group designed the motor drives, a French team developed the doors, a German group designed the

24

electronics and a Spanish team handled the small-geared components. Leveraging global capabilities resulted in a savings of over $10 million in design costs and a 50 percent reduction in development cycle time from 4 to 2 years.

Western European Bloc

Europe 1992 is destroying "Eurosclerosis" and invigorating economic growth. Companies inside and out of Europe are scrambling to respond to the holy grail of European economic integration. A recent study by Richard Baldwin estimates long-term GNP growth will be in the range of 11-35 percent greater with Pan-European harmonization.

East European Bloc

And the wall came tumbling down...

Dramatic events in Eastern Europe, while yet to be completely defined, will certainly provide an impetus for tremendous economic activity. The capital shifts are already sending corporate planners back to their drawing boards to incorporate its impact. For example, western Germany has been the leading foreign investor into Spain based on low wages and opportunities. Much of this direct investment can be expected to flow into eastern Germany which has even lower wages as well as a common language. Additionally, eastern Germany is only 40 percent as productive as western Germany, which translates into enormous economic potential for a united Germany.

Further, German monetary unification will create a driving impetus toward political and economic integration. As a banner outside the eastern German city of Leipzig proclaimed, "If the D-mark comes, we stay. If the D-Mark doesn't come, we go."

While the focus has been primarily on eastern Germany, every nation in the Eastern bloc is teeming with unmet consumer demand and economic potential.

Asian Bloc

However, if you think bringing down the iron curtain was tough, try to scratch the bamboo curtain of Japan.

An Asian trading bloc is being carved out by Japan which focuses on high value-added products and relies on countries like Korea and Malaysia to provide inputs. Of course, "Japanophobia" is an ever-looming threat promulgated by naive politicians and others who proclaim that international trade should be "fair" as defined by them.

Latin American Bloc

In Latin America, the debtor cartel is becoming increasingly vocal about the effect of huge borrowings on the region's standard of living. As an example, Latin America's largest borrower is Brazil with a foreign debt of $114 billion. Brazil has a strong merchandise trade surplus of $16 billion which is offset by interest expense of nearly $15 billion. In short, the cost of debt is becoming politically and socially unacceptable and therefore is everyone's problem. Problems with Less Developed Country (LDC) loans are a prime factor in why few U.S. banks enjoy a AAA-rating, which increases their cost of capital and decreases competitiveness.

North American Bloc

Finally, the U.S.-Canada Free Trade Agreement, designed to eliminate most tariffs by 1994, and all by 1999, has bound the economic destinies of the world's two largest trading partners. The tying of the U.S. and Canada is probably the least controversial and most underestimated of these developing regional trading alliances.

The Debate on Floating Exchange
Rates Continues...

On the macroeconomic level, the debate continues to rage on the effects of flexible exchange rates on everything from social costs and political autonomy to speculative bubbles. It seems, however, that the debate centers on the question, "Do you want to be subject to free market price adjustments or political lobbying?" That is, it is simply a trade off between freely determined market risk and "set in a vacuum" political risk, rather than an elimination of risk per se. Simply put, floating foreign exchange rates provide a continuous forum for a global economic referendum on the fiscal and monetary policies of the world's trading nations. The floating exchange rate regime has provided an economic "shock absorber" to the constant changes and contradictions in the fiscal and monetary policies of the world's trading nations. Whatever your political persuasion, these macro drivers should continue to induce increasing rates of volatility into the value chain and organizational structure of the firm. General and financial managers must be aware of the effects of these drivers on their firm's markets and competitive position.

Microeconomic Drivers:
What Does Higher Currency Market
Volatility Mean to Managers?

How do macroeconomic contradictions and inconsistencies between trading nations impact a firm's ability to survive and prosper? That is, what are the implications and trends for general and financial risk managers to survive and win during the turbulent 1990s? The following microeconomic drivers will provide some insight into the product development trends to consider when designing a proactive financial risk management strategy. Microeconomic drivers refer to specific characteristics and trends impacting the firm's structure and competitive advantage.

27

Higher Adjustment Costs

An important consideration is higher adjustment costs—especially on capital budgeting and other fixed asset decisions which are not easily changed in response to currency fluctuations. For example, building a plant in England to serve the European market may invite export market entry and penetration by U.S. exporters during a period of dollar weakness. The costs of switching production internationally between plants due to exchange rate fluctuations which deviate widely from parity measures is usually untenable because of large fixed costs, labor contracts and the like, which make this option highly undesirable at best.

The costs of production shifting across borders are also exacerbated by the continuing decrease of direct labor costs as a percent of total product cost. At General Motors, for example, direct labor cost accounts for around 25 percent of total cost of a car, and at Toyota and Ford, 18 percent.

Another trend forcing corporate responsiveness and creativity is flexible engineering which is making smaller lot sizes increasingly economic. Grid computer, for example, only produces each portable personal computer to order. In short, computer aided design systems which communicate directly with the shop floor are redefining the term economies of scale. Another interesting example is Mazda whose Miata sportscar model is profitable with a production run of only 40,000 cars annually with a base price of about $13,500. How? Mazda has designed a production system to build multiple models, including the Miata, on the same assembly line.

Not only are small lot sizes forcing quicker customer response times, but concurrent engineering—where marketing, design, engineering and production work together—decreases the product development time it takes to go to market. American Telephone & Telegraph Co., for example, recently decreased its product development cycle time in half from the normal 3 years for a redesign of phone switching computers. In fact, one study credits concurrent engineering programs with decreasing development time 30 to 70 percent, increasing return on assets by 20 to 120 percent and decreasing time to market by 20 to 90 percent.

Higher research and development costs spread over shorter product life cycles are squeezing profit margins. Further, the need to globally market products to justify huge research and development efforts are exacerbated by greater financial market volatility. For example, the 3 major Swiss pharmaceutical producers estimated the development cost of a new product to be between $125 and $150 million. Moreover, the average drug development period ranges between 8 to 12 years. Development costs are also increased due to heavy regulatory burdens. For example, documentation for FDA approval in the U.S. has grown astronomically. In 1940, the average length of a registration document was only 6 pages. In the 1980s, the average drug approval spanned 200,000 pages.

Flexibility and Responsiveness Are the Orders of the Day

These microeconomic trends have forced the need for greater flexibility in pricing products to customers and minimizing the risk profile of long-term cash flows. Speed to market and higher investment costs increase the risks and opportunities in product markets. The treasury staff can no longer afford to quitely contemplate how to beat the market for a few basis points or pips on a competitive bid. Rather, the successful financial risk manager in the 1990s must be a functional expert who proactively recognizes and fulfills his role in the company's value chain. Foreign exchange strategic hedging seeks to achieve this goal by assisting in (1) protecting price fluctuations to customers and suppliers, (2) maintaining profit margins which provide capital for investment and product development, and (3) ultimately, provide for the maximization of long-term cash flow and firm value. As C. Bartlett an S. Ghoshal point out in *Managing Across Borders*, "the challenge of responsiveness is exacerbated by the unpredictable and frequent changes in economic, technological, political, and social   environments. The real challenge is not to be responsive today, but to build the capability to remain responsive as tastes, technologies, regulations, exchange rates and relative prices change."

Figure 1.15 Summary of Forces Driving Strategic Hedging

Macro Forces

- Floating exchange rate regime
- Decoupling of capital market from goods market
- Wide deviations from parity measures
- Globalization and convergence in value in equity market
- Declining role of the U.S. dollar
- Exports redefining economic map
- Global regionalism

Micro Forces

- Higher capital adjustment costs
- Continuing decrease in direct labor costs increases capital intensity
- Flexible production shifting and concurrent engineering
- Higher R & D costs spread over shorter product life cycles

Learning organizations which display the attributes of flexibility and responsiveness will win in the 1990s

2

Defining
Strategic Hedging

"In large scale strategy, when the enemy starts to collapse you must pursue him without letting the chance go. If you fail to take advantage of your enemies' collapse, they may recover.

"In large scale strategy, people are always under the impression that the enemy is strong, and so tends to become cautious. But if you have good soldiers, and if you understand the principles of strategy, and if you know how to beat the enemy, there is nothing to worry about."

—MIYAMOTO MUSASHI, A BOOK OF FIVE RINGS

The efficacy of tactically hedging transactional foreign exchange exposures such as known payables and receivables is a generally accepted industry practice for multinational corporations. For reasons, some valid and others not, the notion and practice of strategic or economic hedging is ambiguous in (1) concept, (2) the regulatory environment in which it operates, and (3) most importantly, practical implementation, measurement and control. There are three different types of exposure to be considered when planning a foreign exchange strategy—transactional, translational and strategic exposure.

- **Transactional exposure** focuses on isolated transactions in the non-functional currency of an operation. Exposures of this type

31

are most often accounts payables or receivables in foreign currencies.

- **Translational exposure** is reflected by changes in balance sheet valuation as a result of currency fluctuations.

- **Strategic foreign exchange hedging** is the systematic positioning of a firm's assets and liabilities towards a long-term objective such as market share or profit margin maintenance. In other words, strategic hedging is concerned with the maximization of competitive advantage and long-term cash flow. Thus, transactional and translational hedging may be seen as subsets of strategic risk management.

Additionally, strategic hedging seeks to better serve the customer by providing stable prices in local currency terms over long periods of time. While foreign exchange strategic hedging does not impact the intrinsic quality of products, it can dramatically impact the value of transactions to customers. Sustainable competitive advantage is a result of total superior value which includes all functional areas— research and development, manufacturing, marketing, finance, and personnel—delivering value-adding goods and services to meet customer needs. These objectives are, of course, necessarily externally oriented, long-term and proactive in nature from a foreign exchange management point of view.

Managing for Competitive Advantage and Firm Value

Strategic hedging, thus, is simply the long-term management of economic or cash flow exposures deriving from foreign currency fluctuations. The problem may be summarized in the following syllogism:

The value of a firm is its discounted cash-flows. Currency fluctuations impact cash-flows. Therefore, currency fluctuations impact shareholder value.

Further, the framework of modern financial theory would also suggest that, all things being equal, strategic hedging should decrease financial risk and increase a firm's value versus a firm which does not hedge. Of course, this will only be true if the marginal costs associated with this approach are outweighed by the marginal benefits actually realized. The challenge may be summed up with the familiar equation:

$$PV = \frac{\Sigma \, (CF)}{(1 + r)^n}$$

Where the present value (PV) of the firm is the sum of expected cash flows (Σ (CF)) discounted at the cost of capital (r) for n periods. It follows that the pursuit of a firm's objectives such as market share, profitability, and capital investments creates a stream of cash flows over time. Whether a firm faces international competition via exports or foreign imports, the cash flows of a firm will be exacerbated with high rates of capital market volatility. Minimizing the volatility or distribution of cash flows, therefore, will necessarily increase a firm's value. Moreover, increasing rates of volatility can place firm survival itself at risk (See Figure 2.1).

The most celebrated example of adverse currency fluctuations driving a firm into bankruptcy is Laker Airlines. The former British concern was literally flying high throughout the 1970s. Increasing pound revenues from frequent flying British travellers induced Laker to purchase five additional DC-10 airplanes. An exposure arose because the purchase was financed in U.S. dollars and revenues were in British pounds. When the dollar strengthened beginning in 1981, the profit margin of Laker Airlines was squeezed through the vicious cycle of lower travel volume because vacationing in the U.S. became

Figure 2.1   Distribution of Firm Cash Flows

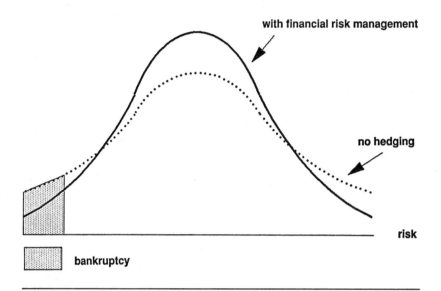

more expensive in British pound terms and higher costs because liabilities were in dollars. These twin shocks induced by British pound devaluation against the U.S. dollar eventually sent Laker Airlines into bankruptcy.

Foreign Exchange Strategic Hedge Planning Cycle

An effective foreign exchange strategic hedging program is not only technically sound, but must also be extremely well understood in concept throughout the company. Establishing a formal planning and review cycle, therefore, provides a framework where various functions can have input and "buy into" the process. The foreign exchange strategic planning cycle includes developing qualitative goals and quantitative objectives, multifunctional analysis, simulation of alternatives, implementation and review.

The firm's strategic plan is the vehicle for establishing foreign exchange objectives. Allowing the reverse can exacerbate, rather than control, the effect of foreign exchange gyrations on the value of a company's cash flow. The strategic objective for foreign exchange programs should be to maintain or achieve competitive advantage, without permitting currency fluctuations to erode market share or profit margins.

For example, the objectives of an American speciality steel firm may include maintaining 25 percent worldwide market share with a return on investment of 15 percent. Assuming the firm's primary competition is Japanese, the fall of the U.S. dollar versus the yen by over 50 percent between 1985 and 1990 would have increased the American company's competitive advantage. The American firm will want to maintain this advantage in order to minimize the competition's ability to raise prices in yen terms leading to (1) a minimization of the competitor's profits, (2) a diminished ability to invest in capacity and new technology, and (3) a reduction in market penetration.

Strategic exposures can also be somewhat hidden from the normal accounts payable and receivable definitions. While the interaction between research and development and currency fluctuations may seem distant at first glance, for example, consider the case of Merck & Co. The U.S.-based pharmaceutical giant earns nearly 40 percent of its $6.6 billion revenues from overseas markets. Merck is faced with a funda-mental strategic exposure—U.S. research and development is funded through worldwide sales of which 40 percent are in foreign currencies. In fact, during the strong dollar period between 1980 to 1985 Merck & Co. attributes a sales decrease of nearly $900 million to unfavorable currency fluctuations. In response, Merck employs long-range foreign exchange options to protect the firm's 5-year planning horizon. Merck's use of long-term currency options is an innovative and proactive approach to protect long range product development which will create the company's future.

Once exposures and strategic objectives are defined, establishing a multifunctional team which examines capital and product market conditions is essential for success. Multifunctional coordination between all elements of the value chain is crucial to a successful hedging program. Strategic business planning for products is the starting point of this coordination. Once the strategic objective of low cost or product differentiation, as well as target markets are defined, the role of foreign exchange can be analyzed.

Traditionally, foreign exchange management followed a sequential approach. That is, strategic planning led to product development which led to production, marketing and the like—and somewhere along the line the treasury department was notified of an exposure. This pattern logically follows from the traditional role of the treasury department of providing funds and cash management, as opposed to being a proactive player during strategy development.

Today's global environment is changing the way firms organize activities in order to increase responsiveness to customer needs and achieve competitive advantage. In fact, concurrent development teams are already redefining the way products are brought to market. Concurrent development is the parallel designing of products and production processes to decrease product cycle time to market. According to a study by McEachron and Tara, concurrent development with multifunctional teams seeks to better serve customers by (1) introducing joint processes and teaming between customers and suppliers, (2) collapsing sequential tasks to parallel or overlapping development, and (3) provides continuous improvements and feedback across functional lines. Since treasury's objective is to support the organizational goals of the firm, it seems a logical extension to support parallel product development which can be severely impacted by foreign exchange rates. As an example of how concurrent development can dramatically impact profits, a recent analysis of the high tech industry showed that the overall profitability of a product which is on schedule and 50 percent over budget will drop 5 percent; whereas the profitability of a product which reaches the market on budget but 6 months late drops by 33 percent.

Multifunctional input should lead to competitive scenarios which may be simulated with varying exchange rate possibilities. Simulations should include an estimate of the short- and long-run demand functions of the firm's goods and services by product line or major market. Additionally, elasticities of demand with respect to foreign exchange rate changes should be developed to assist in monitoring how sensitive the chosen strategy is to constantly changing product and financial markets. In addition, a review of marketing and purchasing conditions facing the firm should be included to qualitatively assess the inherent business risk of foreign exchange hedging strategies. For example, if a firm were 100 percent certain of its sales forecast, hedging with forward contracts would probably be the cheapest method of protection. Unfortunately, transaction costs, volatility, functional substitutes and competition creates an uncertain environment which requires proactive risk management.

The basic dilemma is akin to the type of strategic exposure faced by the savings and loan industry. S&Ls basically have 30-year assets in the form of mortgages and short-term liabilities derived from savings and money market accounts. The S&L industry's strategic exposure is to rising interest rates and/or an interest rate yield curve inversion, either of which would cause a squeeze in margins between fixed interest income from mortgages and floating interest expense from money market accounts and certificates of deposit. Many S&Ls attempted to cover this gap in the 1980s by investing in high yielding junk bonds. Unfortunately, the high default rate in the junk bond market whipsawed the S&L industry into a liquidity crisis which eventually led to a bailout by the federal government. When testifying to the Senate Banking Committee on the estimated $250 to $500 billion cost of the S&L bailout, Federal Reserve Board Chairman Alan Greenspan said "the size of this hole is astronomical."

Strategic foreign exchange exposure is analogous in that a fundamental exposure arises from having the cost of capital on long-term capital assets such as plant, property and equipment being paid for with short-term receivables defined as the company's terms of sale. As an example, a company may have $100 million of capital employed in plant, property and equipment with an expected useful life of 10 years. However, competitive conditions dictate the company's terms of sale to be net 45 days. While the accounting definition of transactional exposure is the net 45 day terms, the firm clearly faces the strategic exposure between using short-term receivables to produce long-term returns on capital employed.

While this position is clearly exacerbated by currency gyrations, it would most probably be imprudent and cost inefficient to hedge cash flows over the plant's useful life of 10 years. Depending on the probability of consummating the sale, the appropriate hedging horizon may be from the current budget year to several years. The efficacy of strategic hedging is thus determined by the integration of currency management into the firm's strategic planning cycle.

The entire strategic planning process itself is by its very nature fraught with uncertainties. Technological obsolescence, natural disasters and the like can throw the best laid plans into a tailspin. Nonetheless, the purpose of strategic planning is to provide a generalized framework for the future direction of the firm. Global competition mixed with high rates of market volatility places strategic currency management at a prominent place in planning considerations.

Foreign exchange strategic hedging may thus be summarized as an attempt to optimize the relationship and disparities between a firm's sales and cost structure versus the competition to achieve competitive advantage. At worst, the goal is to be foreign exchange neutral vis-à-vis competitors; and at best to operatively maintain a long-term competitive advantage induced by foreign exchange fluctuations.

Figure 2.2   Foreign Exchange Strategic Planning Cycle

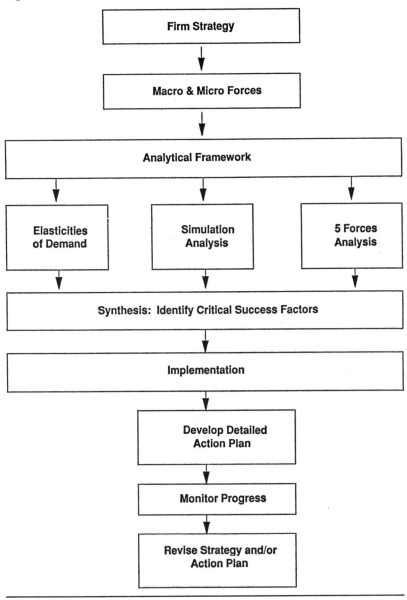

3

Developing the
Analytical Framework

A well developed framework for analyzing the impact of foreign exchange fluctuations on product markets is an essential starting point. The objective of this section is to draw upon tried and true tools from economics to tell a coherent story regarding the risks and opportunities facing the firm as a result of currency gyrations. Once a framework is developed, an example of a U.S. exporter selling into the European Economic Community (EEC) market will be developed.

As a starting point for analysis, we will assume perfect competition exists such that (1) there are many buyers and sellers, where no single player can influence price, (2) the product is homogeneous, (3) there is perfect mobility of resources, and consumers and producers have perfect knowledge. As we will see, relaxing these assumptions (for example, replacing perfect competition with an oligopoly) can alter the degree of the answer, but not the substance.

In a competitive market, the forces of supply and demand determines a product's price. This makes the company a price taker. Thus, a market and firm structure may be summarized in Figure 3.1, where P* represents the market clearing price of a commodity, and therefore, the price a firm can sell its product.

To this familiar framework, we add the classic microeconomic cost structure (see Figure 3.2), where marginal cost (MC) is the total cost per unit change in output; and average variable cost (AVC), average fixed cost (AFC) and average total cost (ATC) complete the company's

41

Figure 3.1 Market and Firm Structure

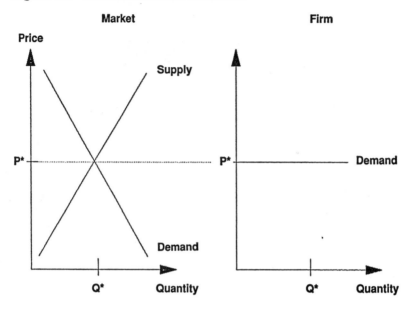

Figure 3.2 Firm Cost Structure

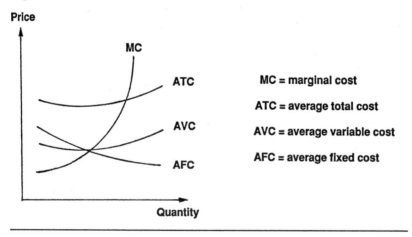

MC = marginal cost

ATC = average total cost

AVC = average variable cost

AFC = average fixed cost

Figure 3.3   Firm Demand Curve Possibilities

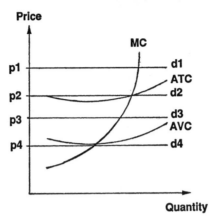

cost structure. It is important to note that ATC = AVC + AFC. For this reason, the rest of the analysis will focus on MC, AVC and ATC. Combining the cost structure curves with demand possibilities facing the company gives the following geometry (Figure 3.3).

At demand curve d1, price is greater than average total cost (ATC) and the company is maximizing total profits. d2 represents the firm's break-even point, where price equals ATC. d3 represents a loss-minimizing structure in which the company is covering variable costs, but not fixed costs, ATC - AVC. d4 represents what economists call the shut down point and what business people call pain, where the company is not even covering variable costs and minimizes losses by stopping production altogether.

With a market demand and cost structure, the next step is to add exchange rate volatility (Figure 3.4), where volatility is determined by the standard deviation (STD) of the foreign exchange rate (E).

Since foreign exchange markets are generally regarded as normally distributed and reasonably efficient, standard deviations around the current rate becomes a powerful analytical tool.

Figure 3.4   Exchange Rate Volatility

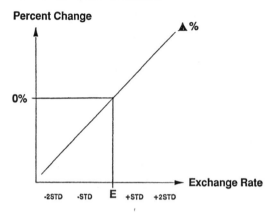

Figure 3.5   World Market, Firm Structure and Exchange Rate Volatility Framework

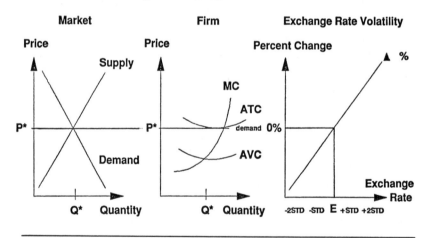

Finally, we combine the world market, a firm and exchange rate volatility into a comprehensive analytical framework (See Figure 3.5).

The Dynamics of Product Markets, Firm Structure, and Exchange Rate Variations

Now we are ready to develop scenarios of foreign exchange variations on a company's product market. As an example, consider a case with the following parameters:

1. The objective is to serve the European Common (EC) market; and customers are sensitive to Deutsche mark (DEM) pricing.
2. Two companies are competing—a U.S. firm and a German firm.
3. The U.S. firm sells exports from the U.S. in DEM, but has 100 percent U.S. dollar costs.
4. 100 percent of the German company's sales and costs are DEM denominated.

This case may be summarized in Figure 3.6.

Since the U.S. exporter is a DEM price taker, a favorable currency fluctuation from DEM/USD* to DEM/USD^1 will increase the effective U.S. dollar price (implying a strengthening of the DEM) to P^1 and raise profit margins accordingly.

If, on the other hand, the DEM weakens from DEM/USD* to DEM/USD^2, the effective U.S. dollar price falls to P^2. Also in this case, P^2 is below the shut down point because the U.S. exporter is not recovering its average variable costs.

The Case of the U.S. Medical and Dental Supplies Market

An illustration of this type of market pattern is the medical and dental supplies market which provides a wide range of diagnostic equipment such as X-ray machines, therapeutic devices such as prostheses, and drug delivery systems such as syringes. Marked by high

Figure 3.6 Exchange Rate Volatility

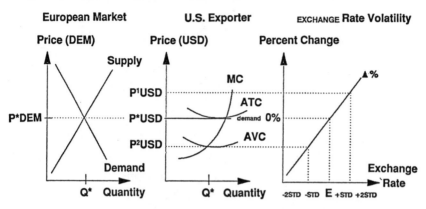

0 At P*DEM=P*USD, the U.S. exporter is recoverring total costs (ATC) and is foreign exchange neutral.
0 At P¹USD, the U.S. exporter benefits from a favorable DEM/USD fluctuation because P*DEM translates into more U.S. dollars.
0 At P²USD, the U.S. exporter loses because P*DEM translates into less U.S. dollars at DEM/USD².

growth and country differentiation in the 1970s, the 1980s were characterized by a decade of cost pressure and rationalization. The main forces in the medical and dental supplies market in the 1990s will be (1) a further trend towards consolidation to decrease distribution costs and increase economies of scale, (2) inpatient markets under tremendous cost containment pressure as shown by the emergence of joint hospital-corporate buyer groups, and (3) a rise in the outpatient market and a decrease in inpatient stays.

The medical and dental supplies market has effectively globalized and is dominated by the U.S., Germany and Japan. U.S. manufacturers earn one-third of their earnings from international sales. The fall of the U.S. dollar from March 1985 has translated into double-digit export growth, which rose U.S. exports 22 percent to $3.9 billion in 1988 alone. Exports in 1989 were estimated to have increased by 13 percent to $4.4 billion. The rise in exports enabled the United States to register

46

a trade surplus of $1.2 billion in 1988, which represents an increase of 71 percent from 1987.

Of interest is that successful players in the medical and dental supplies market are being called upon to provide product differentiation and be low-cost producers simultaneously. Differentiating through the introduction of new product technology while being under cost containment pressure is causing increased industry consolidation. Hospitals, for example, still use the acquisition of new technology to lure the best doctors. At the same time, the hospitals are forming purchasing cartels to squeeze price concessions from medical equipment producers. These trends have resulted in making the attainment of economies of scale a precondition of economic survival due to high research and development costs. In recent years, for example, the U.S. prostheses sector has narrowed to only 7 firms providing over 50 percent of world production.

Figure 3.7   U.S. Medical and Dental Supply Trade Surplus and U.S. Dollar Index (1978–1987)

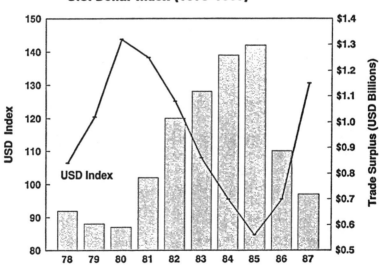

Economies of production will be further enhanced with the harmonization of medical device standards and regulations in the European Community under 1992 negotiations.

Further, industry globalization is also pushed by regulatory forces such as the proposed Medical Device Improvements Act of 1988 now in the U.S. House of Representatives. The bill aims to create a safety and recall system similar to the U.S. automobile industry.

The medical and dental supplies market is thus characterized by intense global competition, high research and development costs, and well informed customers with strong buying power. It is no wonder why the industry is so sensitive to currency fluctuations—markets are simply lost at the margin. As Figure 3.7 shows, U.S. medical and dental suppliers are world price takers. In fact, during the 1980s each 1 percent increase or decrease in the trade-weighted dollar has cost or benefited medical and dental supply producers $21 million of market share.

4

Elasticities of Demand and Exchange Rates

In the preceding section, a major assumption is that prices fully respond to currency movements. In the real world, however, the adjustment of demand to price changes depends on the elasticity of demand. The elasticity of demand is simply a measure of the responsiveness of demand with respect to a change in price. The elasticity of demand may be expressed as:

$$\text{Price Elasticity} = \frac{\%\ \text{Change in Quantity}}{\%\ \text{Change in Price}} = \frac{\Delta Q}{\Delta P}$$

There are three states of elasticity: unitary, elastic, and inelastic (See Figure 4.1). Unitary elasticity occurs when a 1 percent change in price causes a 1 percent change in demand. Demand is said to be elastic when a 1 percent price change causes a more than 1 percent change in demand. And inelastic demand occurs in a market in which a 1 percent change in price causes a less than 1 percent change in demand.

In general, elasticity is an increasing function of product homogeneity. For example, Belgian lace and Bohemian crystal would be very price inelastic because no substitutes exist. On the other hand, commodities such as gold, oil and soybeans are very price elastic because an ingot of Russian 24 kt gold is the same as Canadian 24 kt gold.

49

Figure 4.1   Elastic, Inelastic and Unitary Demand Curves

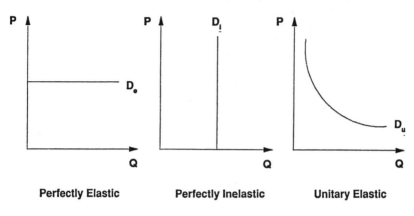

| Perfectly Elastic | Perfectly Inelastic | Unitary Elastic |

When prices simultaneously adjust to currency movements, the "law of one price" is said to hold.

Most products, of course, fall in the "in between" category. As was shown in the previous chapter, the medical and dental instruments market was quite elastic with respect to exchange rate movements, yet X-ray machines certainly do not qualify as a commodity! In general, the elasticity of demand with respect to foreign exchange rate changes is simply a variation of the familiar price elasticity formula:

$$\text{Foreign Exchange Price Elasticity} = \frac{\%\ \text{Change in Demand}}{\%\ \text{Change Foreign Exchange Rate}}$$

In a study on the exchange rate responsiveness of U.S. industry performance, J. Ceglowski found demand elasticities to be significant in a number of American markets. She found that "the real exchange rate is a significant factor in both exports and imports of textiles, apparel, lumber, furniture, paper, chemicals, rubber and plastics, stone, clay, glass, electrical machinery and instruments." Further, a number of industries were found to be highly elastic where "a 1 percent increase in the rate of real depreciation would both raise the export growth rate and lower the import growth rate of textiles, apparel, lumber, and furniture by about 2 percent."

An interesting example of the impact of foreign exchange rate elasticity on a global market is the textile industry. Kanebo, the world's largest textile group based in Japan, attributed a 16 percent decrease in the company's return on sales to a 50 percent strengthening of the yen from 1985 to 1990. In the face of strong global competition, Kanebo was precluded from raising prices when the yen strengthened. As the market leader, Kanebo truly competes in a global market with geographically dispersed players.

Five Largest International Textile Groups in 1988

Rank	Company	Country	Sales (USD Billions)
1.	Kanebo	Japan	$3.9
2.	Coats	UK	$3.4
3.	Armstrong	U.S.	$2.8
4.	Chargeurs	France	$2.8
5.	Milliken	U.S.	$2.6

Adding to Kanebo's woes, import penetration of foreign textiles into the Japanese market increased by 37 percent during this period. This resulted in a major restructuring which forced the company out of viscose production, caused the closure of its Hofu plant, and a merging of a series of production facilities.

Cross Elasticity of Demand and Foreign Exchange Rates

Currency fluctuations also impact the cross price elasticity of demand. In currency terms, this allows the relative price of substitutes to change due to exchange rate changes. For example, Molson, Canada's largest brewer, reported 1989 sales were "up 3 percent, but overall results were depressed by a 4 percent gain in the Canadian dollar." Molson's dilemma is one faced by many firms—"Do we give up profit margins or market share?" However, not only is Molson exposed to American and European beers, but also to substitutes such as French wine and Scandanavian vodka which decreases in Canadian dollar terms with a strengthening currency. Thus, foreign exchange cross elasticity of demand in this example may summarized in the following formula where a percentage change in the price of Canadian beer impacts the demand for French wine.

$$\frac{\text{Foreign Exchange}}{\text{Cross Elasticity}} = \frac{\%\text{ Change in Demand for French Wine}}{\%\text{ Change Price of Canadian Beer}}$$

Thus, if cross elasticity were unity, a 5 percent strengthening of the Canadian dollar versus the French franc will cause a 5 percent decrease in beer sales and a 5 percent increase in French wine sales.

"We Don't Have Any Exposure Because We Sell in U.S. Dollars" Syndrome

While it is commonly thought that the elasticity of demand with respect to exchange rate changes is an increasing function of product homogeneity, many U.S. firms have ignored foreign exchange exposure by implementing the "we don't have any exposure because we sell in dollars" approach. This approach is dangerous because it obfuscates the effect and accountability of managers for the impact of currency fluctuations on profitability. Why? Because in order to be responsive to customer needs, the U.S. exporter must be sensitive to the price foreign customers pay in their local currencies. Moreover, pricing exports only in dollars (1) adds an additional burden on a

Figure 4.2 Oil Price Indices (1973–1990)

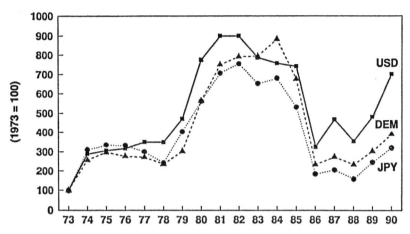

customer's buying criteria, (2) deviates from product quality and service discussions, and (3) raises the threat that a manageable financial issue could harm customer relations. In the case of oil producers selling into Japan, for example, the amount of Japanese yen per metric ton determines customer demand—regardless of how many U.S. dollars comprises the cost of sales (See Figure 4.2). Removing currency issues is not a panacea for product quality, but it does increase the value of the total transaction (by decreasing the customer's risk of purchasing from a foreign source).

A recent study by Michael Knetter also showed that the price elasticity of demand is, among other factors, a function of the level of a country's exports as a percentage of total output. German exporters, for example, were found to stabilize U.S. market prices in dollar terms; whereas U.S. exporters are characteristically passing through exchange rate changes to the importer. This suggests that U.S. exporters are not typically sensitive to the effect of U.S. dollar pricing on the customer. This makes U.S. sourcing relatively riskier and, therefore, less desirable. This disturbing conclusion points to the need for American multinationals to have greater responsiveness and sensitivity with regards to the effect of currency fluctuations on the price foreign customers pay.

Why Elasticity Matters

As long as elasticity is positive, currency gyrations will force a trade-off between maintaining relative market share position and protecting profit margins (Figure 4.3).

A recent study by Froot and Klemperer showed something that Japanese businessmen have intuitively practiced for years—that is, the more concentrated an industry is (what economists call oligopoly) the more maintaining current market share will impact future profitability. This means that as industries consolidate, market share will become increasingly difficult to obtain and maintain. As a corollary, secular shocks due to financial market gyrations create either opportunities or risk of firm survival at an increasing rate.

Figure 4.3 FX Fluctuations Force Trade-offs Between Market Share and Profitability

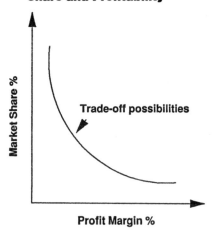

5

Simulating Strategic Alternatives

"Doubt is not a pleasant condition, but certainty is an absurd one."

—VOLTAIRE, *FREDRICK THE GREAT*

"We have the right to fail, but let's only fail once in a row."

—THOMAS D. MIGNANELLI, CEO, NISSAN USA

The simulation of most likely, optimistic, and worst case scenarios is a well accepted tool of strategic planning and analysis. With microcomputer and spreadsheet analysis, simulations provide a ready vehicle to test underlying economic and business assumptions to changes in currency markets. The strengths and weaknesses of the underlying business place a given simulation in the context of a firm's relative competitive advantage. Therefore, it is absolutely essential to employ a balance between the firm's qualitative market power with suppliers and customers to the quantitative orientation of simulation analysis.

Five Forces Industry Analysis and Foreign Exchange Rates

Five forces industry analysis places the firm's competitive position within the context of managerial judgement and represents a qualitative benchmark for consensus building across functional lines (See Figure 5.1). This analytical tool, popularized by M. Porter et al., seeks to describe industry attractiveness and competitive rivalry as a function of barriers to entry, supplier and customer bargaining power, and the threat of substitutes.

- **Industry attractiveness** is an overall assessment of the market and its future outlook. For example, the market for plastic disposable diapers may have a low industry attractiveness rating due to consumer activism regarding the environmental damage of non-biodegradable products. On the other hand, the market for geriatric medicine may be perceived as attractive with the average population age increasing due to longer lifespans.

- **Competitive rivalry** forms the nexus of the five forces analysis. The level of competitive rivalry is a measure of market concentration. For example, the world market for nickel—which is principally used for stainless steel production — is principally controlled by Inco and Falconbridge of Canada.

- **Barriers to entry** are comprised of economies of scale, regulations, tariff rates, and other means by which potential competitors are impeded from market entry. For example, start-up costs for an automobile manufacturing facility which could efficiently produce competitively priced cars would undoubtedly be a multimillion dollar investment.

- The **threat of functional substitutes** can be a very difficult force to gage because it is usually a matter of degree rather than kind. For example, European consumers may prefer a California chardonnay over a French chardonnay at today's price. However, a 25 percent appreciation of the U.S. dollar versus the French franc may cause only a segment of budding sommeliers to switch over to French wine. Further, a 50 percent appreciation of the U.S. dollar may cause nearly all Europeans to drink French wine.

- The **bargaining power of customers** is another important force bearing on competitive rivalry. For example, the large Japanese conglomerates known collectively as the *zaibatsu* are known to pressure medium sized suppliers into extremely tight quality standards, just-in-time inventory management, and liberal credit terms—all of which adds to intense rivalry among suppliers to firms such as Honda and Toyota.

- A parallel force is the **bargaining power of suppliers**. For example, the bargaining power of diamond merchants over DeBeers diamonds is quite negligible due to the latter's near monopoly position over the world diamond market.

Figure 5.1 Five Forces Industry Analysis

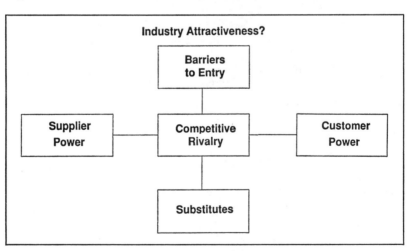

Simulation Analysis

From a qualitative five forces analysis (Figure 5.1), the next step is to construct a quantitative simulation analysis. The starting point of simulation analysis is the base case forecast. As an example, a hypothetical American firm named Yankee Globex Corporation (YGC) will be analyzed for a foreign exchange strategic hedge.

There are five steps in constructing a strategic hedge simulation analysis—(1) develop a forecast, (2) determine the exposure, (3) quantify the hedging variables and associated costs, (4) determine statistical market characteristics, and (5) simulate alternatives.

Table 5.1   Yankee Globex Inc. (U.S. Dollars Millions)

STEP 1				TOTAL FY	PERCENT OF
SALES	FY 1991 FORECAST	FY 1992 FORECAST	FY 1993 FORECAST	1991-1993 FORECAST	TOTAL SALES
U.S. dollars (USD)	$33.3	$33.3	$33.3	$100.0	33.3%
German marks (DEM)	$33.3	$33.3	$33.3	$100.0	33.3%
Japanese yen (JPY)	$33.3	$33.3	$33.3	$100.0	33.3%
TOTAL SALES	$100.0	$100.0	$100.0	$300.0	
COSTS					
U.S. dollars (USD)	($90.0)	($90.0)	($90.0)	($270.0)	-90.0%
PROFIT	$10.0	$10.0	$10.0	$30.0	10.0%
STEP 2					
EXPOSURE					
German marks (DEM)	$33.3	$33.3	$33.3	$100.0	
Japanese yen (JPY)	$33.3	$33.3	$33.3	$100.0	
Total Exposure	$66.7	$66.7	$66.7	$200.0	

Step 1 (see Table 5.1) is obtaining YGC's 3-year forecast for which the functional currency is the U.S. dollar. Further, all costs are incurred in U.S. dollars with sales evenly spread among U.S. dollars (USD), German marks (DEM), and Japanese yen (JPY).

Step 2 (also see Table 5.1) summarizes YGC's foreign exchange cash flow exposure which, in this case, is comprised of JPY and DEM sales. YGC's USD sales, however, are also exposed because a weakening yen or mark versus the dollar would allow an opportunity for Japanese and German competitors to lower prices in dollar terms without sacrificing profit margins in their respective functional currencies.

Once the base case is established, the mix of hedging instruments can be constructed with the three basic building blocks of currency management—(1) forwards, (2) options and (3) wu-wei.

Characteristics of Forwards

Forwards: A foreign exchange forward contract is an agreement to buy or sell foreign currencies for delivery at a future date at an established exchange rate.

Some characteristics of foreign exchange forward contracts are as follows:

- Foreign exchange risk is fully protected at the forward rate.
- The buyer and seller are obligated to deliver currencies at maturity or to offset the contract prior to maturity.
- Forward rates are typically available for periods up to 5 years for major currencies. However, the markets tend to lose liquidity after 2–3 years which tends to increase costs.
- Forward exchange rates are determined by adjusting spot rates by the appropriate forward discounts or premiums. Forward premiums and discounts are determined by interest rate differentials between two currencies as well as the forces of supply and demand. High (low) interest rate currencies will trade at a forward discount (premium) against low interest rate currencies.

- The cost of a forward contract is implicitly factored into the forward contract rate. This is shown as the difference between the spot and forward exchange rates.

Characteristics of Options

Options: A foreign currency option is the right, but not the obligation, to buy (call contract) or sell (put contract) a given amount of currency at an established exchange rate (strike or exercise price) at or before an expiration date. An option is distinct from a forward in that the latter requires that the given transaction be effected on the value date.

The following are some characteristics of options:

- There are two parties in an option contract: the option seller (writer or grantor of right) and option buyer (holder of right).
- Options are valid until the maturity or expiration date. An option that can be exercised at any time through maturity is termed an American option. An option that can be exercised only at maturity is termed a European option. At maturity, the option holder can exercise the right to buy or sell, let the option expire, or sell the option in the market.
- The buyer pays an upfront fee known as an option premium to the seller. The premium is expressed as U.S. cents per foreign currency unit or as a percentage of the strike price. Options are quoted in-the-money (strike price below market price), at-the-money (strike price equals market price), or out-of-the-money (strike price above market price).
- The price of an option is a function of:

    Intrinsic Value: This is the differential between the spot rate and strike price at any point in time.
    Time Value: The more time the contract has to expiration, the greater chance it has to become profitable. For increased time and risk, the writer will charge a higher premium.

Volatility: This is the measure of a currency's stability. A unit that rarely moves will certainly carry far less risk for the writer than one which gyrates wildly. As a corollary, the buyer of an option prefers more volatility than less because the probability of expiring in-the-money also increases with larger market movements. For pricing purposes, volatility is measured as the annualized standard deviation of a given currency's percentage change over time.

Interest Rate Differential: This is the spread between the interest rates of the two currencies concerned for the period until expiration.

Options are available in most major currencies up to 5 years. The market tends to lose liquidity, and thus result in higher prices, beyond 2-3 years.

Characteristics of Wu-wei

Wu-wei or Do Nothing: It is not an oxymoron to assert that the alternative of doing nothing is not taken seriously enough in the sense of being an active and deliberate decision. In America we say "don't just sit there, do something!" However, there is a Buddhist expression, wu-wei, which means "don't just sit there, do nothing!" The moral? If you're going to do nothing, do it actively! In foreign exchange terms, doing nothing may be the optimal position if the product is a monopoly or the probability distribution of sales is too wide to forecast.

Continuing with the example, since the functional currency of Yankee Globex is the U.S. dollar, the company's German and Japanese sales are exposed to currency fluctuations. Step 3 (see Table 5.2) reveals alternative hedging instruments and their associated costs.

The next phase is to develop a framework for simulating the effect of exchange rate changes on Japanese and German sales. In the case of YGC yen and mark sales, the simulation begins with the spot rate and extends by 3 standard deviations in either direction (See Figure 5.2).

61

Table 5.2 Yankee Globex Inc. (U.S. Dollars Millions)

STEP 3

HEDGING VARIABLES	SPOT	+1 YEAR	+2 YEARS	+3 YEARS	AVERAGE
DEM/USD	1.670	1.668	1.658	1.645	1.657
FORWARD DISCOUNT					
(PREMIUM)		-0.0024	-0.0115	-0.0250	-0.0130
FORWARD SALE GAIN					
(COST) %		0.14%	0.69%	1.52%	0.79%
PUT OPTION COST %		-4.04%	-5.34%	-6.10%	-5.16%
VOLATILITY %		11.00%	11.15%	11.30%	11.15%
JPY/USD	158.00	155.71	151.40	147.00	151.37
FORWARD DISCOUNT					
(PREMIUM)		-2.29	-6.60	-11.00	-6.63
FORWARD SALE GAIN					
(COST) %		1.47%	4.36%	7.48%	4.44%
PUT OPTION COST %		-3.30%	-4.40%	-5.08%	-4.26%
VOLATILITY %		9.00%	9.20%	9.40%	9.20%

Figure 5.2 Normal Distribution

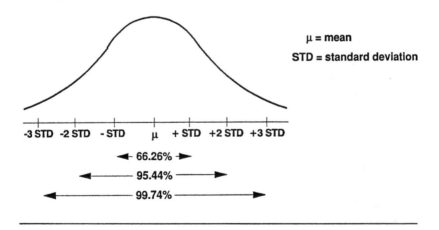

μ = mean

STD = standard deviation

-3 STD -2 STD - STD μ + STD +2 STD +3 STD

66.26%

95.44%

99.74%

Table 5.3 Yankee Globex, Inc. (U.S. Dollars Millions)

STEP 4	YEAR	DEM/USD	JPY/USD	JPY/DEM
	73	2.70	280.0	103.6
	74	2.41	301.0	124.9
	75	2.62	305.1	116.4
	76	2.36	292.8	123.9
	77	2.11	240.0	114.0
	78	1.83	194.6	106.5
	79	1.73	239.7	138.4
	80	1.96	203.0	103.6
	81	2.25	219.9	97.5
	82	2.38	235.0	98.9
	83	2.72	232.2	85.2
	84	3.15	251.1	79.8
	85	2.46	200.5	81.5
	86	1.94	159.1	82.0
	87	1.58	123.5	78.1
	88	1.78	125.8	70.7
	89	1.70	143.4	84.5
	AVERAGE	2.22	220.4	99.4
	MAXIMUM	3.15	305.1	138.4
	MINIMUM	1.58	123.5	70.7
	STANDARD DEVIATION (STD)	0.43	56.3	18.9
	STANDARD DEVIATION (STD) %	19.2%	25.5%	19.0%
	PURCHASING POWER PARITY (PPP)	.74	221.92	127.5
	INTEREST RATE PARITY (IRP)	2.22	188.41	84.9

The assumption of a normally distributed exchange rate regime allows for the construction of a relatively straightforward simulation analysis. Specifically, a normal distribution allows a probability to be assigned to a range of currency changes. Currency fluctuations will occur 68.26 percent of the time between plus or minus one standard deviation, 95.44 percent of the time between plus or minus two standard deviations, and 99.74 percent of the time between plus or minus three standard deviation from the mean.

Table 5.4 Yankee Globex, Inc. (U.S. Dollars Millions)

STEP 5

SIMULATION OF HEDGING ALTERNATIVES

	-3 STD	-2STD	-1STD	SPOT	+1 STD	+2 STD	+3 STD
DEM/USD	0.71	1.03	1.35	1.67	1.99	2.31	2.63
% CHANGE FROM SPOT	-57.6%	-38.4%	-19.2%	0.0%	19.2%	38.4%	57.6%
SPOT	$100.0	$100.0	$100.0	$100.0	$100.0	$100.0	$100.0
FORWARD	$100.8	$100.8	$100.8	$100.8	$100.8	$100.8	$100.8
OPTION	$94.8	$94.8	$94.8	$94.8	$114.0	$133.2	$152.4
DO NOTHING	$42.4	$61.6	$80.8	$100.0	$119.2	$138.4	$157.6
JPY/USD	36.91	77.28	117.64	158.00	198.36	238.72	279.09
% CHANGE FROM SPOT	-76.6%	-51.1%	-25.5%	0.0%	25.5%	51.1%	76.6%
SPOT	$100.0	$100.0	$100.0	$100.0	$100.0	$100.0	$100.0
FORWARD	$104.4	$104.4	$104.4	$104.4	$104.4	$104.4	$104.4
OPTION	$95.7	$95.7	$95.7	$95.7	$121.3	$146.8	$172.4
DO NOTHING	$23.4	$48.9	$74.5	$100.0	$125.5	$151.1	$176.6

Figure 5.3   Yankee Globex Inc. Strategic Hedge Simulation for Japenese Yen Exposure

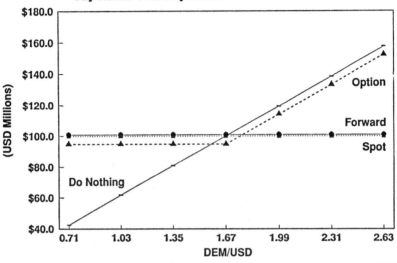

Figure 5.4   Yankee Globex Inc. Strategic Hedge Simulation for Deutsche Mark Exposure

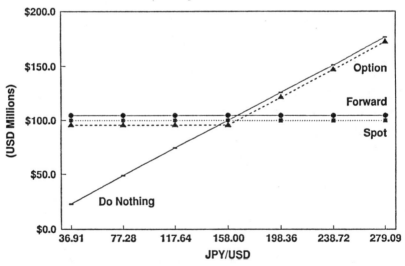

Figure 5.5 Simulation Analysis Summary

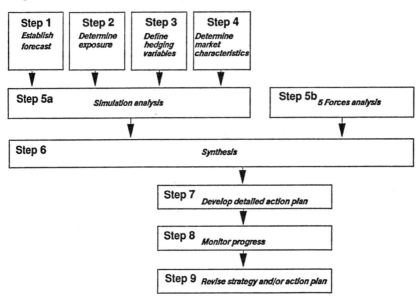

Step 4 (Table 5.3) is to determine exchange rate market characteristics with such descriptive statistics as standard deviations, Purchasing Power Parity (PPP) and Interest Rate Parity (IRP). In this case, the annual standard deviation of the JPY/USD is JPY 56.3 or 25.5 percent; and the DEM/USD is DEM 0.43 or 19.4 percent. Further, versus the spot rates of DEM 1.67/USD and JPY 158.0/USD, the current Purchasing Power Parity is DEM 1.74/USD and JPY 221.9/USD; and the current Interest Rate Parity is DEM 2.22/USD and JPY 188.4/USD respectively.

Step 5 (Table 5.4) is to combine forecasted exposure, hedging variables and market characteristics into simulation analyses. The simulation should quantify the values of exposures at (1) spot, (2) forward, (3) option, (4) do nothing or wu-wei, (5) purchasing power parity and (6) interest rate parity around statistical probabilities.

One of the most interesting revelations about strategic hedging simulation is the lack of precision in arriving at the "right" answer. Why? The juxtaposition between the certainty of the exposure and transaction costs produce a need for a qualitative judgement to be made regarding quantitative hedging alternatives. If the product line of Yankee Globex was very difficult to forecast such as rocket engines, for example, the appropriate hedging vehicle may be a combination of options and doing nothing. On the other hand, products with more stable demand patterns such as commodity chemicals, which are quite vulnerable to the effects of currency swings on price, may be hedged with more confidence (See Figure 5.5).

The Japanese Yen Parallax: The Case of Caterpillar versus Komatsu

Caterpillar Inc. is faced with a strategic foreign exchange exposure which may be described as parallactic. A parallax occurs when the same object is apparently dislocated when measured from two separate points. In this case, Caterpillar Inc. faces a completely different exposure than its primary competitor—Japan-based Komatsu. Exchange rate fluctuations have had a profound impact on Caterpillar's profits to date. In fact, the following graph reveals that Caterpillar's elasticity of worldwide profits with respect to exchange rate changes have been quite material. Between 1982 and 1989, inclusively, Caterpillar's worldwide profits changed 4 percent for every 1 percent change in the Japanese yen/U.S. dollar rate (See Figure 5.6 and Table 5.2).

Caterpillar is a global industry leader in the manufacture of earthmoving, construction and materials handling machinery. The company is also focused on the long-term as evidenced by aggressive research and development expenditures of $387 million and capital additions of $984 million in 1989 alone. The company's attention

Figure 5.6   Caterpillar: Profit on Sales and Exchange Rates Changes (1982–1989)

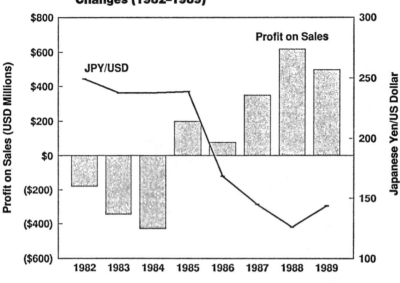

to manufacturing excellence has clearly paid off as evidenced by Caterpillar being ranked in the top 10 in a quality survey conducted by *Fortune* magazine.

Since Caterpillar first began manufacturing overseas in England in the 1950s, the company's operations are nearly equally divided between the U.S. and overseas locations. The company manufacturers in 16 U.S.-based plants and 15 international facilities. Caterpillar's distribution system provides for an even wider global dispersion of products. Caterpillar products are sold and serviced by a worldwide network of 216 dealers serving customers in over 150 countries.

The company is, however, decidedly U.S.-based—in terms of employee concentration and costs, 69 percent or 41,979 of its 60,409 worldwide employees are in the United States. The company attributes exports to supporting over 18,000 direct jobs and a $1.6 billion net contribution to the U.S. trade balance.

Table 5.2   Caterpillar Inc.

	Sales (USD MILL)	Sales Outside U.S. (USD MILL)	% Sales Outside U.S.	Profit On Sales (USD MILL)	Profit % On Sales	Average JPY/USD
1979	$7,618	$4,114	54%	492	6.5%	219.1
1980	$8,603	$4,904	57%	565	6.6%	226.7
1981	$9,160	$5,221	57%	579	6.3%	220.5
1982	$6,472	$3,689	57%	-180	-2.8%	249.1
1983	$5,429	$2,497	46%	-345	-6.4%	237.5
1984	$6,597	$2,771	42%	-428	-6.5%	237.5
1985	$6,760	$2,974	44%	198	2.9%	238.5
1986	$7,380	$3,395	46%	76	1.0%	168.5
1987	$8,294	$3,981	48%	350	4.2%	144.6
1988	$10,435	$5,218	50%	616	5.9%	125.9
1989	$11,126	$5,897	53%	497	4.5%	143.5
Average	$7,989	$4,060	50%	$220	2.0%	201.0
Minimum	$5,429	$2,497	42%	($428)	-6.5%	125.9
Maximum	$11,126	$5,897	57%	$616	6.6%	249.1
Standard Deviation	$1,665	$1,072	5%	$368	4.8%	43.6

Sources: Catepillar 1989 Annual Report and IMF

Caterpillar is also reorganizing itself into a more responsive and focused global player. Its current strategic plan calls for a transformation from an essentially functional orientation to a multiple profit center organizational structure. The company is splitting into 14 different profit centers with an emphasis towards flattening the organizational chart, pushing down decision making and more sharply defining accountability.

Caterpillar is placed within the framework of a five forces analysis below (See Figure 5.7).

- *Industry attractiveness*: Moderate to high because (1) the worldwide prospects for peace and declining defense spending should allow governments to appropriate funds towards badly needed infrastructure spending such as airports and highways, and (2) the growing emphasis on waste disposal should open up new opportunities for Caterpillar products.
- *Competitive rivalry*: High due to intense rivalry with Komatsu of Japan as shown by very elastic worldwide profitability with respect to exchange rate changes versus the yen.
- Barriers to entry: High due to size of fixed investment in producing heavy machinery.
- *Functional substitutes*: Low especially in the earthmoving sector at present. However, the engine, parts and components sector are vulnerable to a high number of competitors worldwide.
- *Bargaining power of customers*: High because Caterpillar sells high ticket items which are typically purchased by government agencies or large companies. Thus, many sales are a result of open tenders which increases the company's price sensitivity.
- *Bargaining power of suppliers*: Low to moderate because most of Caterpillar's suppliers are smaller firms with non-proprietary technologies. The company's wide supplier base is illustrated by the fact that over 1,000 suppliers are in Caterpillar's Quality Assured Certification (QAC) program covering over 80 percent of procured material.

Figure 5.6   Five Forces Industry Analysis for Caterpillar, Inc.

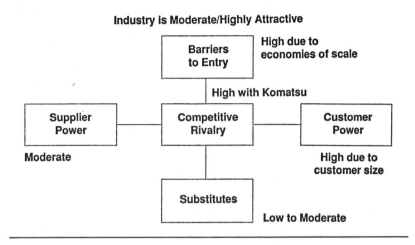

Industry is Moderate/Highly Attractive

A 1982 Harvard Business Review article by M. Porter, T. Hout and E. Rudden on the characteristics of global companies cited Caterpillar as an example of a company that "...has maintained its position against Komatsu and gained market share. The two companies increasingly dominate the market vis-à-vis competitors, who compete on a domestic or regional basis."

The authors designated four characteristics which established Caterpillar as a dominant global player in the heavy equipment manufacturing industry. First, Caterpillar maintains an integrated global strategy which put Komatsu in a relatively weaker competitive position. Second, the company's top management has shown a commitment to invest in manufacturing systems to exploit its global positioning. Third, Caterpillar has consistently invested more capital per employee than Komatsu. Fourth, Caterpillar has also sought a preemptive strike on Komatsu by forming a joint venture with Mitsubishi in Japan which places their competitor in a defensive posture.

Since 1982, Caterpillar has certainly employed an aggressive posture in globalizing operations. However, the company has been uncharacteristically passive in managing foreign exchange exposure. While Caterpillar officials certainly acknowledge the firm's exposure, the response has been focused on lobbying Congress and other political constituencies for a lower dollar. In a *Wall Street Journal* interview, Caterpillar's treasurer stated, "we do not extensively hedge our foreign exchange exposure."

Caterpillar's 1989 annual report noted "unfavorable exchange rates also threaten the U.S. manufacturing sector. We're concerned about the use of an overvalued dollar as an anti-inflation device. Companies like Caterpillar have already endured one severe and prolonged currency-related downturn this past decade. A second could cause severe damage."

Caterpillar's $7 billion per year of foreign exchange exposure, however, would probably be better optimized by a strategic hedging program rather than a political lobbying effort. In 1989 alone, the company's net cash flow before foreign exchange impact was $130 million and only $74 million (or a loss of $56 million) after foreign exchange losses. The company's sensitivity and inaction to Japanese yen fluctuations threatens Caterpillar's highly prized investment program and unnecessarily leaves the company's flank exposed.

6

Organizing For Strategic Hedging: The Paradox of Centralization

"Unfortunately, the financial analysis is all too often "pinned on" afterward, rather like the tail on the donkey in the children's game. An interactive process that relates the product market specifics to the wider financial implications is not only a requirement for sound strategic investment decisions but also a powerful source of organizational learning."

—P. BARWISE, P. MARSH AND R. WENSLEY
"Must Finance and Strategy Clash?",
Harvard Business Review

Successfully managing foreign exchange risk in the 1990s requires accepting the paradox of centralization (See Figure 6.1). This paradox occurs because while managing foreign exchange requires both tactical and strategic excellence, the two modes often have a distinctly different focus.

On one hand, for example, most pundits would argue that centralizing of foreign exchange transactional hedging yields benefits of netting exposures across subsidiaries, provides for control of cash and risk, and drives cost savings due to economies of scale in average transaction size. Tactical hedging is treasury department-specific and

73

Figure 6.1   Paradox of Centralization

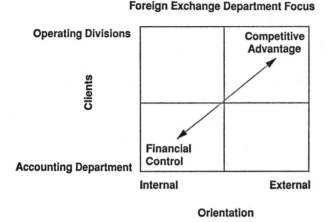

necessarily internally focused. It also makes general managers less concerned about the effects of currency gyrations on their product markets because it creates a syndrome of "the treasury department handles that stuff". Indeed, many U.S. corporations do not hold their general managers accountable for the effect of foreign currency movements on sales. Instead, currency markets are seen as beyond the control of the marketing or sales manager, for example.

On the other hand, strategic hedging is externally focused on the impact of foreign exchange fluctuations on the competitive advantage of the firm. Strategic hedging is thus necessarily externally focused on product markets and on developing responses to the dynamics of competitor behavior.

Towards a Global Model

The primary difference between tactical and strategic hedging is that strategic hedging is absolutely dependent upon multifunctional coordination. As Michael Porter noted, "today's game of global strategy seems increasingly to be a game of coordination—getting dispersed production facilities, research and development, marketing and finance activities to truly work together...successful international competitors in the future will be those who can seek out competitive advantages from global configuration/coordination anywhere in the value chain, and overcome the organizational barriers to exploiting them."

While the organization of an effective foreign exchange strategic hedging program seems somewhat difficult because it necessarily forces the need for multifunctional coordination, companies are already well ahead in combining talents beyond the multinational model.

In the multinational model, subsidiaries are looked upon as a portfolio of assets from which their respective return on investments aggregate to firm value. In this model, achieving economies of scale to meet national needs were emphasized over flexibility. Further, international subsidiaries were usually looked upon as extensions of the parent company, rather than partners, who provide research and development, marketing oversight and production technology.

The global or transnational model popularized by M. Porter, C. Bartlett and S. Ghoshal and others stresses the simultaneous achievement of "...global efficiency, national responsiveness and the ability to develop and exploit knowledge on a worldwide basis." While these three goals may seem inherently contradictory, like the paradox of foreign exchange centralization, transnational companies overcome and exploit these characteristics to create and sustain long term competitive advantage (See Figure 6.2).

While the major difference between the multinational and global organizational models is one of mentality, it also has a conceptual counterpart in finance known as covariance. In financial theory, the existence of different risk classes for assets such as stocks in a portfolio decreases the overall risk profile due to the covariance of returns. In the same way, the global organizational model emphasizes synergies in producing more value than the sum of its parts. For example, Bic

Figure 6.2 International Organizations

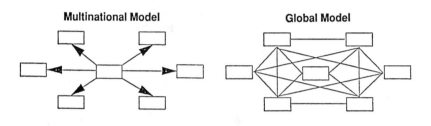

pen developed its worldwide domination of the ballpoint pen market by cross subsidizing production from its European base. Specifically, the firm leveraged its strong position in France to aggressively enter the British market where it accepted low margins to gain a dominant market share position. Once Bic gained a dominant position in the U.K. and other European markets, the company proceeded to the U.S. where it again accepted low margins which were cross subsidized by its strong European position. Competitors who concentrated on local markets were relatively helpless in preventing Bic from gaining a dominant worldwide market. Bic was thus able to leverage an existing business base to create more worldwide value than the sum of its parts.

Bic's aggressive use of crossborder leveraging is also an excellent example of how strategic foreign exchange management could support the firm's objectives. Bic's exposure was first between continental European currencies and the British pound during the U.K. assault phase; then, Bic's exposure was to the U.S. dollar during the U.S. market penetration phase. In both phases of market penetration, Bic went with a high risk strategy of using profits in one country to subsidize accepting lower margins to gain market share. Sharp exchange rate movements could have easily inflicted painful losses during market penetration thereby exacerbating an already risky business strategy.

The role of the foreign exchange team is to organize itself within the firm's value chain to (1) lower the risk of implementing global strategies, (2) ensure the firm is foreign exchange neutral at worst and "locks in" a competitive advantage at best, and (3) provides education and analysis of currency markets to management. This role is best described within the concept of foreign exchange strategic hedging which provides the vehicle for proactively and comprehensively managing the impact of currency fluctuations on firm value and competitive advantage.

Does a Proactive Approach Mean Speculation?

One of the most difficult dilemmas to solve is reconciling the difference between being proactive in risk management and speculation. Many managers incorrectly assert,"We're a manufacturing company, not a bank." This statement often leads to the misguided conclusion that financial risk management should be organized and implemented along primarily defensive lines. If the old raison d'être of a firm was to deliver products, the new imperative for the 1990s is to deliver value systems to meet customer needs. For example, a car buyer is not simply purchasing an automobile, but rather acquiring a transportation system. Today's discerning auto consumer wants superb styling, high quality, safety, fair pricing, and decent treatment on the showroom floor. Nissan's Infiniti auto line is more than luxury sedans. Every aspect of Infiniti from a low-key marketing approach to customer warranties have been painstakingly orchestrated to deliver a high value-added transportation experience. Maintaining stable prices in local currency terms is an important component of delivering total value to customers cited by the Japan-based firm.

Nonetheless, perhaps the most challenging aspect of strategic hedging is overcoming organizational barriers. Specifically, multifunctional coordination and matrix organizations require enormous energy, time and commitment from the implementing company. While many multinationals are involved with international businesses, the commitment to a fully integrated global organizational matrix is lacking in most companies—and the difference between involvement and commitment is crucial. Brazilians have a saying that a chicken is involved in breakfast by contributing an egg, but a pig is committed to breakfast by giving an arm! In short, the globalization of a firm and the commitment of its strategic response in foreign exchange, as in all functional areas, must be absolute for progress to be made.

Moreover, the risk manager must take the lead in providing an educational environment where diverse functional managers can learn about the effects of foreign currency risk on product markets. The focus should be to create cross functional synergy which leads to the incorporation of financial risk management alternatives from the inception of the business planning process. In a recent article on creating organizations that learn, W. Kiechel noted "best of all, [learning organizations] light a way toward prospering in the 1990s and beyond, when the name of the game will no longer be minimizing risks, staying on plan, and making your numbers. Instead, it will become coping with, and capitalizing on uncertainty."

It should also be noted that strategic planning is not an end in itself. As London Business School chairman Peter Williamson recently remarked on the importance of "managing strategically, rather than doing strategic planning...Competitive advantage comes from strategies which do something different than conventional wisdom."

Thus, the main difference between a defensive posture and a proactive approach to financial risk management is mentality. History is replete with examples of defensive approaches which lulled leaders into a false sense of security. Perhaps the most adept at exploiting this weakness and opportunity was General Patton, who said of defensive strategies:

"Pacifists would do well to study the Siegfried and Maginot Lines, remembering that these defenses were forced; that Troy fell; that the walls of Hadrian succumbed; that the Great Wall of China was futile; and that, by the same token, the mighty seas which are alleged to defend us can also be circumnavigated by a resolute and ingenious opponent. In war, the only sure defense is offense, and the efficiency of offense depends on the warlike souls of those conducting it."

PART TWO

Companies and Competition: Excellence in Managing Financial Risk

7

Compaq Computer Corporation

We've worked very hard on communication . . . In each case, our marketing team forecasted and observed what demand was, and we met weekly to discuss the ability of the plants to produce the product and the ability of the distribution centers to ship the product. That flexibility paid off . . . We are always developing contingency plans. We always have a plan A, plan B, and it's not unusual to have plan C. Going back a number of years, obviously, when MCA came out, the analysts wrote us off. The market assumed that plan A was for us to do MCA. Instead, we introduced EISA. That's the best example of our flexibility. Since then, we've more than doubled the size of our organization when many analysts said it wasn't going to happen . . . The Compaq philsophy has always been to do what makes sense, and to be able to change your mind if it doesn't. Running foreign exchange that way required an individual who had lots of experience changing his mind.

—Ben K. Wells,
Manager of Foreign Exchange
Compaq Computer Corporation

Figure 7.1   Performance in Review:
Compaq Computer Corporation (1983-1989)

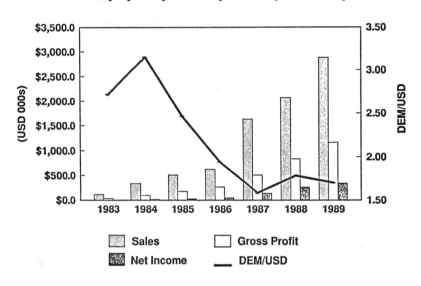

Source: Compaq Computer Corp. Annual Reports

Compaq's Strategic Edge:
Higher Average Selling Price

Ben K. Wells, Manager of Foreign Exchange for Compaq Computer Corp., the Houston-based computer manufacturer, joined the company in June 1987. Before Compaq, he traded in a profit-driven foreign exchange operation at Standard Oil of Ohio (SOHIO) and helped launch BP Finance International's foreign exchange trading operation after BP's acquisition. He also managed currency risk for Carborundum Corp. directly out of school, after receiving his MBA from Canisius College in Buffalo. Included in Wells' background is the quantitative and mathematical grounding of an in economics major at

84

Table 7.1 Performance in Review: Compaq Computer Corporation
Income Statement (U.S. Dollars in Millions)

	1983	1984	1985	1986	1987	1988	1989	Avg.	CAGR %
+ Sales	$111	$329	$504	$625	$1,224	$2,066	$2,876	$1,105	72.0%
– Cost of Goods Sold	($105)	($305)	($442)	($525)	($968)	($1,657)	($2,301)	($900)	67.2%
Gross Profit	$6	$24	$61	$101	$256	$409	$575	$205	113.9%
Gross Profit %	5.4%	7.3%	12.2%	16.1%	20.9%	19.8%	20.0%	14.5%	24.4%
– Depreciation	($1)	($4)	($9)	($15)	($22)	($49)	($84)	($26)	97.9%
– Other Income & Costs	$0	($3)	($8)	($12)	($8)	$7	($7)	($4)	
PBT	$5	$16	$44	$74	$225	$367	$484	$174	115.7%
– Taxes	($2)	($4)	($17)	($31)	($92)	($119)	($165)	($61)	104.5%
Taxes %	-46.9%	-21.5%	-39.2%	-41.7%	-40.8%	-32.5%	-34.1%	-36.7%	-5.2%
Net Income	$3	$13	$27	$43	$133	$248	$319	$112	123.6%
Net Income %	2.3%	3.9%	5.3%	6.9%	10.9%	12.0%	11.1%	7.5%	30.0%
Working Capital	$75	$68	$140	$141	$338	$635	$749	$307	46.8%
Working Capital/Sales %	67.4%	20.6%	27.9%	22.6%	27.6%	30.7%	26.0%	31.8%	-14.7%
Long-term Debt	$0	$0	$75	$73	$149	$275	$274	$121	
Long-term Debt/Sales %	0.0%	0.0%	14.9%	11.6%	12.2%	13.3%	9.5%	8.8%	
Earnings Per Share	$0.07	$0.24	$0.45	$0.67	$1.75	$3.05	$3.73	$1.42	94.0%
Cash Flow Per Share	$0.08	$0.33	$0.68	$1.06	$2.28	$3.86	$5.14	$1.92	100.1%
Average Annual P/E	0.0	14.5	10.8	11.7	12.7	8.9	11.3	10.0	

the University of Missouri, which he attended as an undergraduate student, and an M.S. in economics from Texas A&M.

Compaq's timing couldn't have been better. In 1987, it had reached the $1 billion sales mark faster than any other start-up company after initiating shipments to international markets in 1984. In 1986, international demand for Compaq products tripled and accounted for 17 percent of total revenues. By 1987, non-U.S. revenues had grown to 24 percent of total sales. A weak dollar allowed much of its growth to come from European markets, where superior price/performance characteristics made Compaq the fourth largest computer company in only five years. Sales in Europe and other international markets contributed 45 percent of Compaq's overall revenues in 1989 and 54 percent in 1990. International sales, principally in Europe, grew 62 percent in 1989 over 1988 and exceeded $1 billion in annual revenue for the first time.

As sales were exploding in the mid-1980s, however, senior management also grew concerned that a strong dollar could hurt the company's earnings in overseas markets. Working in foreign exchange markets since 1978, Wells was hired. Although Wells' strategies are now risk-averse, he is given flexibility at Compaq to overhedge or underhedge transactional exposures associated with costs and revenues denominated in foreign currencies. He thus takes market views regularly, using financial instruments such as forwards, options, and combinations of these two instruments to design hedging strategies that fit Compaq's overall risk profile. According to Wells, for example, tactical purchases of put options on European currencies in 1988 allowed Compaq to take advantage of a strong dollar. As a result, net income for that period was not materially affected.

Despite such success, Compaq's greatest challenges may be yet to come. Since 1982, Compaq has designed personal computers (PCs) to be compatible with IBM's standard PC architecture, while making a niche for itself by increasing the power and speed of the PCs it designs. This has proven to be a very profitable stategy for Compaq, with sales, net income, and earnings per share reaching record levels from 1987 to 1990.

In April 1987, IBM strategically announced that it was building a new line of personal computers from scratch—the Personal System/2—with internal computer architecture called microchannel architecture (MCA). MCA was specifically a change in the size and electrical configuration of the slots used for add-on boards, and did not allow the use of standard PC add-on boards and peripherals such as modems, expanded memory, enhanced graphic boards, and network adapter cards.

While many analysts predicted the death of Compaq and other IBM competitors, Compaq successfully accepted the challenge. The company has spent $254 million on research and development, employing 1,400 R&D staff to counter the challenge. In September 1988, Compaq and eight other manufacturers announced the Extended Industry Standard Architecture (EISA), an extension to the industry standard bus design which can also accommodate high performance 32-bit expansion boards. In November 1989, Compaq released the COMPAQ SYSTEMPRO and COMPAQ DESKPRO 486/25, each of which incorporates EISA. EISA has permitted Compaq to deliver significant high-performance capabilities to personal computer users while maintaining full compatibility with an installed base of more than 30 million PC users.

The COMPAQ DESKPRO 486/25, based upon Intel's 486 microprocessor, takes advantage of the EISA bus, delivers 15 million instructions per second ("MIPS") and offers up to three times the performance of 25-MHz 386 based computers. The COMPAQ SYSTEMPRO features a tower design and is the first PC system to support multiprocessing tasks and operations. With 8 to 40 MIPS of computing power—depending on product configuration and number of processors—it delivers performance that is comparable to minicomputer class systems. It is also the first PC system to offer drive array technology—previously found only in mainframes—which delivers significantly higher disk subsystem performance than standard PC products. This computer specifically offers a price-performance advantage.

From its inception, Compaq has challenged IBM by emphasizing the quality, reliability, additional features, and full functionality of its products. As the personal computer marketplace has developed, Compaq has concentrated its efforts in the high-performance niche of the personal computer marketplace, focusing on business and professional users and developing products with greater functionality and more competitive features.

Another challenge lies ahead for Compaq which could make managing currency risk even more important. The high-performance end of the personal computer market now competes directly with the computer workstation and minicomputer markets in an increased number of professional applications such as engineering. In addition, recent developments in workstation products have made them increasingly competitive with mincomputers on the higher end and personal computers on the lower end. The workstation market is highly competitive and new technology comes out of R&D departments regularly. Many of the recent advances by competitors in this market have been based upon reduced instruction set computing (RISC) which, under certain circumstances, enables machines to process data faster than computers based upon complex instruction set computing (CISC) and simplifies the development of a larger base of software applications. Compaq's products, like other personal computers, are based upon CISC technology. An increased number of software products designed for RISC machines utilizing UNIX operating system have become available and RISC machines may come to dominate the workstation market. While Compaq currently markets CISC machines capable of employing the UNIX operating sytem, this could create price pressure on existing computer technology.

Compaq, however, continues to pursue a strategy in which the features of its products are more important factors than price in the purchasing decisions of target markets. In 1989, it achieved revenue and earnings increases in spite of competition from lower-priced

Figure 7.2   The Economics of Downsizing

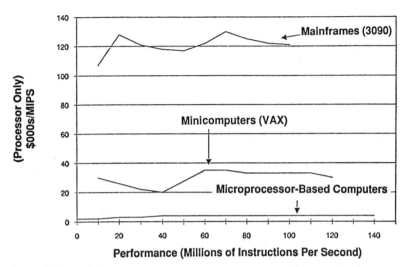

Source: Goldman Sachs

personal computers introduced by other manufacturers (so-called "clones") and price reductions by IBM and Apple Computer, Inc.

With price competitiveness and product differentiation now becoming an even more serious issue in the computer industry, Compaq must continue to introduce new technology that offers features beyond those of competitors in order to continue exploiting the industry's downsizing trend.

According to Daniel C. Benton, an analyst at Goldman Sachs, the computer industry trend towards downsizing is inescapable—and Compaq could be a big winner. The reason? As shown in Figure 7.2, cost per million instructions per second (MIPS) is clearly in favor of companies such as Compaq. Cost per MIPS for a mainframe is approximately $120,000, for a mini computer $35,000, and for a micro computer less than $5,000. As Benton explains: "Clearly, the price/

performance of microprocessor-based computers far outstrips that of traditional mainframes and minicomputers. Furthermore, the absolute performance of microprocessor-based systems can now exceed that of mainframes as multiple microprocessors are combined in a single computer system."

In a nutshell, the increased power of Compaq's new technology—such as the SYSTEMPRO—will allow it to continue to go after other computer markets with higher average selling prices (ASPs). Adds Benton: "Unlike IBM, Compaq can participate in the downsizing trend without hurting ASPs. Given current ASPs of just over $3,000, sales of SYSTEMPROS, with prices ranging from $20,000 to $50,000, will increase the company's gross margin and lead to greater profitablity."

As Wells points out, however, Compaq must also pay attention to another factor that poses a threat to both profit margins and revenues—foreign currency risk—if it expects to continue growing at its current pace. At the time this interview was conducted, Compaq marketed its products in 62 countries and manufactured in the U.S., Scotland, and Singapore. Products were primarily sold in the U.S., Europe, Canada, Australia, and New Zealand, with additional markets being established in Southeast Asia, Latin America, and South America.

Interview: Ben K. Wells

Ben, can you explain why the world is now a riskier place for Compaq?

Wells: It's pretty simple. Our exposure is bigger. We have had a ten-fold increase in our exposure to currency risk as a result of revenue growth in three years.

Where does this ten-fold increase come from?

Wells: Principally from Europe. We are still a predominately Europe-looking organization.

What about establishing greater penetration in Asia?

Wells: We've announced that we are going to be opening up organizations in the Pacific Rim. We already exist in Australia and New Zealand, and we have operations in Japan that are growing.

And how specifically do you manage the currency risks associated with an increasingly European revenue base, and foreign sourcing of computer parts?

Wells: Basically, we are risk-averse. What perhaps differentiates us from some other companies is that we are very aggressive in managing our exposures. In Compaq-ese, we do what makes sense, with an emphasis on maximizing our flexibility. If what we've done in the past doesn't make sense now, then we stop doing it. This philosophy has worked well for us.

An executive of a German car manufacturer recently told me that a 10 percent strengthening of the Deutschemark against the dollar has significantly impacted his company. He doubted that any car manufacturer earns a 10 percent margin on the cars it sells. Is that true of companies such as Compaq as well, and the computer industry overall?

Wells: The analogy doesn't really hold for us. We are still primarily a dollar-based industry. In this way, we are not that dissimilar from an oil company. And we don't, right now, share the same risks that a global car company would. So it would be very difficult for me to come up with a story to highlight a similar problem.

What we can say, with a ten-fold increase in revenues, is that obviously any impact from a currency move is potentially ten times bigger than what it was at one point in time. In 1987, we generated

$600 million in revenues. Now we are at around $3 billion, more or less.

So what's your role specifically in addressing this exposure?

Wells: I am the point man, so to speak, who pulls the trigger. But Compaq is very much a team-oriented, consensus-oriented company, so I am not alone. While I may be the guy that follows the markets daily, we are always working the issue as a team. Four or five people are involved in the process.

At some companies you will find an assistant treasurer who only devotes part of his time to the foreign exchange problem, yet this is your job full-time?

Wells: The perception I get from other institutions and other companies is that this is a part-time job for some organizations, and for a few individuals. But Compaq feels that it's an important enough area that it has devoted two individuals to the task, and 100 percent of their time is spent studying these markets. Our job is managing currency risk, period.

So to whom do you report to on your activities?

Wells: I report to the treasurer, Neel Foster, and he reports to the CFO, Daryl White, who reports to the president and chief operating officer.
They ultimately keep the controller and our board appraised of market dynamics that we are facing and allow them to evaluate our overall performance.

What special skills do you need to do your job?

Wells: I've got an analytical background, because my educational days were heavily spiced with math and statistics, which has helped a lot. Without being facetious, I think you have to be a quantitative person to do this. More importantly, I'm truly interested in what I do. This is a job you can't be ambivalent about. I learn something everyday and enjoy that.

As far as skills and personality traits, you almost have to have a temper. I've never met a good risk manager who is also laid back. I guess that's because the best risk managers have always had a quick response time—call it a temper, call it reaction time, call it an ability to think on your feet. You can't get confused in this job, because the markets are confusing enough. If you cannot handle more than two inputs at a time, you are probably not very good at this.

I've got two phones and an assistant that keeps yelling at me. I am a phone hound, always seeing what people think. Maybe they have a thought that I haven't had. On the days it's busy, I may be talking to two people more or less simultaneously, and having a third person yelling at me, telling me who she is talking with, and what they are saying. You have to be able to digest that information and hopefully move in a correct manner.

How frequently does management review your performance?

Wells: We differentiate ourselves again from other corporations in this regard. We measure our performance on a monthly basis. Everyone sees it on a monthly basis, including the treasurer and CFO obviously, and anyone above them on demand. We run a performance model which evaluates our performance on a daily basis, and we have discussions about our activities on a monthly basis. So senior management is very much involved in how well my staff and I are performing. We are definitely not operating alone.

What sort of end-of-the-year review do you do, and what goals might your area have?

Wells: I am measured on the performance of two models. One that turns monthly, and one that turns annually. One takes a look at the short run, and one takes a look at the long run in this business—a year being what I call the long run. The models evaluate how I've done over the time frames in question. There are no set goals. I am just expected to perform well.

If there are reasons why I haven't, given the inter-year review process that we do every month, this will come to light. We will have set the team in place, and we will have an action plan to address the currency problems we face. So the end of year is like any other month here really.

Why's that?

Wells: The management of risk is done in such a dynamic or fluid environment, as anyone in the business knows. Here it's given a lot of serious thought continuously. We operate here on the basis of no surprises, so a year-end review would be redundant based on everything we do monthly.

What percentage of your sales is done overseas?

Wells: That's real hard to say. It's very fluid. It's somewhere around 50 percent. But one thing I've learned here is that the computer business fluctuates just about as quickly as exchange rate prices.

Very fluid? What are the extremes?

Wells: Between 50 percent to 60 percent is a good range.

Would you characterize your firm as following a product strategy of low cost or differentiation?

Wells: Definitely differentiation. Differentiation would describe our product strategy. To use the car analogy that didn't work before, we are definitely in the BMW or Mercedes class. We view ourselves as a world-class differentiated manufacturer.

Who are your major competitors?

Wells: IBM might be one, and Apple might be another. The rest are taken all very seriously as well. We take everyone seriously. And we are constantly evaluating where we stand—that's what marketing is all about.

Do you ever get involved from a decision-making point of view in choosing your manufacturing locations based on currency issues as well?

Wells: That is part and parcel of the Compaq team approach, so the answer is sure. We have three plants, in three different countries—our Houston plant, being our largest, followed by Scotland, or more correctly the U.K. for exposure purposes, and Singapore.

Plant locations have got a shopping bag full of critical events, if you will, that determine whether we manufacture in one place or another.

Can you pull out the top five?

Wells: I would guess you could go to Europe—the U.K., France, and Germany. The major EC players are our major markets. But actually I should point out that that has made my job a little bit easier because I have not had to deal with problems I have had in the past such as blocked currencies. Much in the Compaq tradition, they thought out very thoroughly where they have gone. The results have been, if you will, an easier risk management job than it could have been. If we were sitting here with South American exposure, that would be one difficult issue to deal with.

If you had been at Compaq in 1985, do you think they would have reacted any differently to the strong dollar?

Wells: I'm not sure we could have acted any differently in 1985, because keep in mind we were only three years old. Even when I came here in 1987, the risk profile was just evolving.

Obviously, we've stated in the past that the dollar's decline has made it easier to do business in a lot of different areas. But we were very comfortable with a strategy in place to manage the movement at the time, and we view our business as one of not speculating in the markets, but of managing risk. In hindsight it's easy to observe that the dollar's decline from 1985 was perhaps uni-directional, but you didn't know that at the time. Basically, our strategy was to take advantage of the dollar's decline, and to protect ourselves from the upside, in case it reversed itself. Anytime you do that you give up some of the advantages of the dollar's decline. I can't believe I would have been comfortable with any other approach. The approach we took was very rational.

What is your most significant sourcing exposure?

Wells: I guess the highly publicized chip shortages two years ago. We have a very aggressive purchasing organization, and again the Compaq team was aware of the shortages as they started evolving. We didn't experience some of the highly publicized problems that other organizations incurred as a result. We didn't do anything different. We just managed through the situation.

Fortunately, a lot of these significant price and risk exposures just don't happen over night. They evolve. If your team is functioning in a well-oiled manner, and truly working, then there are no surprises. The chip shortage and the dollar's decline, as well as the dollar's subsequent rebounding in 1989—we managed around them all.

What exactly was your approach to managing currency risk during these times, and why was it effective?

Wells: We've worked very hard on communication—on knowing what the left hand and the right hand are doing. In each case, our marketing team forecasted and observed what demand was, and we met weekly to discuss the ability of the plants to produce the product and the ability of the distribution centers to ship the product. That flexibility paid off.

We are always developing contingency plans. We always have a plan A, plan B, and it's not unusual to have plan C. Going back a number of years, obviously, when MCA came out, the analysts wrote us off. The market assumed that plan A was for us to do MCA. Instead, we introduced EISA. That's the best example of our flexibility. Since then, we've more than doubled the size of our organization when many analysts said it wasn't going to happen.

Why did Compaq hire you?

Wells: I came here in 1987. But the currency exposure had started evolving in 1985 and 1986. The strong dollar was a perceived risk. Management felt it would be unconscionable to leave it alone. They wanted to put brackets around it, to contain it.

Did you face any roadblocks when you arrived in 1987 and started to deal with the exposure?

Wells: I don't want to make this look like a risk manager's paradise, but I didn't have to endure a great deal of indifference. It was a breath of fresh air for me personally coming here.

Why do you think they specifcally hired you? You came from a very active, bank-oriented corporate risk management program?

Wells: You're right. Before this, my job was primarily to speculate. The real issue here was the way they felt they wanted to structure their risk management program. The Compaq philsophy has always been to do what makes sense, and to be able to change your mind if it doesn't. Running foreign exchange that way required an individual who had lots of experience changing his mind. In the speculative environment, you truly change your mind and think on your feet. A lot of strategies out there are buy and hold—and go down with the ship. That's not a strategy Compaq employs.

Doesn't sound as if you ran into much resistance?

Wells: I've had a lot of encouragement. If I've needed something and could make a rational argument for it, I've had little resistance.

What's an example of that?

Wells: There are a multitude of examples. When I came here, for example, they didn't have a complete set of informational tools which I felt were necessary to properly manage the exposure. Unless we had the proper informational flows, we weren't going to be successful.

We brought in all the screens and information systems we needed. I have as much information as I had when I worked in the speculative environment, and I have more information than some banks. That's the most visible type of encouragement I've received.

What other support have you received?

Wells: Management has a very open view as to which institutions I wanted to deal with. They wanted an individual who was familiar with a large spectrum of institutions. I was thus able to develop those relationships. In addition, they also let me have a hand in developing a risk management policy. In other words, I didn't run into the that's-not-the-way-we-do-it syndrome.

Why do you think that was the case?

Wells: Compaq is a well-managed company. It's that simple. We had a really interesting information management system, and it allowed me to develop computer models to track our exposures on a daily basis. That tracking ability has only been enhanced over time, as our models have become more sophisticated and far-reaching. These models basically allow me to tell what has been shipped from Scotland, from Singapore, from Houston, Germany, France, and Holland, yesterday and today. I know our exposure first thing every morning. That kind of informational flow is critical in this business, in my opinion.

I always hear that is a problem.

Wells: It can be. I know what that is like, because I have also lived through those information deficient kind of environments. At Compaq, it was recognized that this was a risk. And we had a series of meetings with a number of individuals, worked those issues, and made it work. To be honest, that's the easiest part of my job here. It's so unbelievably easy on the receivables side.

On the obligation side, our purchasing people have signed up with the program as well, and I am regularly included at the inception of contract negotiations. So I know when the exposures are being created. Since then, we have developed new computer systems that would cope with that as well.

We may spend a lot of time on exposure management, but not a lot of time doing the same task-oriented things. At Compaq, we don't have a lot of excess staff. And it's important for us to get it down once and mechanize it, so we can get on with our jobs. In fact, I'll be honest with you, I can no longer sympathize, I can only empathize with other corporations. I have been quickly forgetting what it's like not to have a good grip on my exposures.

What has made your system that way?

Wells: A lot of old line companies say they are computerized, but the question is—to what extent and how well. Basically, when I presented my problems, I was able to go to our information management group and they gave me a solution. Within six months, I was on-line and operating. So, it's really the culture, the environment in which I'm operating.

How does the culture differ from what you find at other companies?

Wells: Compaq trusts the foreign exchange manager to make the best decisions. Every trader is expected to create a risk/reward ratio based on market conditions and the problems he's facing. He is expected to do what makes sense, not to make stupid bets. For existing situations that reoccur—for example, selling in Germany—we have a very set program under which the trader operates.

On the other hand, when new exposures arise—for example, a new contract with some vendor or something along those lines—the team concept comes into play. Management, however, has worked the issues beforehand, so the trader's responsibility is to implement solutions.

After all, when something new happens in the market, you can't continue to do the same thing. We reconvene the team and consider the alternatives. That team involves the controller, CFO, treasurer, all of whom make themselves readily accessible.

Basically, that's how we decide to adjust our positions. If we execute a hedging program and something changes, there are no penalties for being right and then wrong. There's not a lot of one upsmanship. I have no fear of going back and saying, 'This is what the team decided to do based on such and such discussions, but now it's all wrong. Can we change it?' They expect that, if you will. That gives us the two-way flow, to allow our risk managment program to work.

Can you talk anecdotally about that process. Obviously, not all of your decisions are going to be perfect?

Wells: There have been a lot of times since I've been here that it has happened, but the most eventful to me—because it was the very first time it happened—was in November 1987. Up to September or October that year, the dollar had been starting to appreciate. I started getting vibes that the dollar was getting ready to crater.

I went to my boss, and said, 'This will get real lonely if I'm sitting on all these hedges which protect us from the dollar going up, and the dollar absolutely craters. We will not be able to benefit from the advantages that would normally come if we were the other way.' He said, 'Let's get some people on the phone.' Basically within 15 minutes, we made a strategic decision to alter our hedging program to take advantage of what we perceived to be the next move in the market. As fate would have it, I was right that time. The market did really work the dollar over and drive it down. Fortunately, Compaq enjoyed the bulk of that move.

And what financial tools do you use to make such hedging decisions and adjustments?

Wells: We could talk on that subject forever. But basically, the tools and strategies that we use are not unique. Nothing is unique at Compaq, in a sense. We keep it very simple. One of the hallmarks of my risk management style is to keep it simple. By keeping it simple, I find two fundamental factors come to the fore quickly. Seriously, a simple strategy is more likely to work than a more complex strategy. If something is complex, I'm usually very leary, because I don't know how rigorous the strategy is. If the market doesn't behave in the

the same manner you thought it would, you've got a mess on your hands.

Second, I have to go to the team and explain the strategy that I've employed. If I can't explain it in 25 words or less, I've got people from various disciplines who will not buy off on it. That's a real problem. I have found more risk management programs that got into trouble because no one trusted the individual in question—there was always that persistent doubt.

I have worked very hard to explain to Daryl White [Compaq's Senior Vice President, Finance, and CFO] what I'm doing, and he understands. As a result, he can walk into the board meeting and talk about the subject, and they can walk away understanding what we've done. If I've been able to do that, I believe I have done my job.

I use all the strategies and tools, but I probably don't get carried away to the extent that I'm doing something exciting. I don't use those types of strategies here. When an option applies, an option is used. When a forward applies, a forward is used. And when a combination applies, a combination is used.

And how is your performance evaluated?

Wells: With the help of our performance models. It basically goes out and takes our exposures and runs a hypothetical hedge of 100 percent—that is, completely square, no exposure. After it operates, I'm evaluated against the performance models.

Explain how you present concepts to, say, your CFO or board.

Wells: I'm being paid to be in tune with the market and know the risk/reward ratios. What I traditionally have done is go to management and review the alternatives. Everyone of them has a risk/reward ratio pasted to it—a payoff, a downside, an upside, a matrix of possibilities.

If the team feels that the forward contract is more to their liking, then that's what we do. It's human nature for your risk profile to change, so as your company gets larger and becomes more successful and your products are more readily accepted worldwide, it's only logical for risk profiles to perhaps change. These sessions allows me to know their risk profile.

But if I say, 'Look, I've got a butterfly straddle here,' everyone would give me a funny look. That only serves to confuse. If I do something 'complex,' I break it down into its components and risk/reward ratios. I might talk to people in the market about butterfly spreads, but I'll be darn if I will go into a team meeting and talk about it.

Do accounting conventions affect your risk management program?

Wells: Of course. That's how the outside world measures Compaq's performance. At the same time, do I ignore economic exposure? No. So the answer is yes and no, really.

We do have to be sensitive to what accounting conventions dictate, because whether we like it or not, that's how the financial community and our customers measure Compaq. At the same time, we try not to be myopic. We try to look over the hill, because they are also expecting us to be here next year, the year after, and long after that. So therefore, in tune with our attempt to be well-managed and well- controlled, we are always looking ahead at what our economic exposures may or may not be.

So what types of exposures will you hedge?

Wells: All of our subsidiaries have a functional currency of the U.S. dollar. That means certain things to us from an accounting perspective. And we are very much a believer here that translational exposures are real exposures for our business, and we work that issue. We hedge those. We also believe that transactional exposures are very real, and we work those. As far as strategic exposures, that's an ongoing discussion item. Compaq continues to review that issue.

Can you share your views about strategic hedging?

Wells: This whole thing about strategic and economic hedging may be overstated. We view 'strategic hedging' as simply doing what makes sense. And if you are going to cause more harm than good, then logic would tell you not to. That's something that we continue to work on and discuss. Strategic exposure can come from many different avenues, especially in the small computer market. Price is a strategic issue—whether or not your product is in the commodity basin, which we don't feel they are. But that could become a strategic issue. Technology could shift, much as it did on the 80/86 issue. That's a commodity business now, and technology is always a strategic issue. Product development is a strategic issue.

All I can say is there is a lot of thought as to whether treasury is the right forum to address those issues.

Can you give me a clue where you side on that now? Should it be part of the solution?

Wells: To be fair to the team, we haven't reached a consensus yet.

What's unique about your program?

Wells: Compaq's risk management systems, its team approach, the overall culture, and the general trust Compaq places in its employees.

An example of this? Some corporations require anywhere from two to three signatures before a position is eliminated or hedged, but anyone who deals in the market knows that it can change in a second. By the time you've gotten your third signature, you could have been creamed.

Compaq's systems allow me to know what our postions are at 7:00 A.M. in the morning. The team approach is already hashed out at that time—as well as the strategies that are to be employed. Compaq then trusts me to implement those to the best of my ability, based on what the team has developed as its consensus. As a result, I've got any number of ways that I can jump that would be acceptable, and hopefully if I'm right on the market, would be appropriate to hedging Compaq's exposures. That openness and teamwork gives us the flexibility we need to have for a successful program.

Discuss a specific strategy that has worked in the past, that might be exemplary of the types of things you do to hedge risk?

Wells: I can tell you of one strategy that we use on the receivables side. As I said, Compaq's style is to underhedge or overhedge within certain parameters, and that's why we've been successful. The parameters are percentages of exposure. But what this allows me to do is anticipate the market. If the dollar is going up, it doesn't make a lot of sense for me to be sitting around being cool, and saying, 'Hey, I'm hedged,' and then find out tomorrow that I'm underhedged. So they allow me to anticipate the market moves. Couple that with an ability to change my mind, and Compaq gives me a lot of latitude in the market. Obviously, that allows me to be overhedged or underhedged, either short or long, and allows me to change my mind.

Most importantly, what that allows me to do is keep those institutions honest that prey on people in the markets who show their sides. I make it very risky for them to do that with me. This allows me to act in the company's best interest 90 percent of the time.

If you can go long or short, what links it back to an objective of 100 percent hedged?

Wells: Obviously, they have that benchmark measurement from which to judge our performance all the time.

So what makes management reconsider a decision you've made if you make a mistake?

Wells: Keep in mind that I'm not in a vacuum. The treasurer gets daily reports, senior management monthly. I have to be perfectly honest: it's never happened to me that I've been on a real run where I keep getting beat up ad infinitum, and lose on my bets. Logically, if I were to have a bad streak [against a 100 percent hedged benchmark], then there would be a reconvening and they would talk about the strategies we are employing.

Back in 1987, and a couple of times since, I have gone back to management and said, 'If we continue to do X, Y is going to happen to us.' I have tried very hard to anticipate their concerns, in other words.

Obviously, I'm not telling you I've guessed the market right for three straight years, because that's ludicrous. I haven't. What I am saying, when I've been wrong, is that the treasurer and other people see the results daily and they know where things stand.

In the open culture we've developed, it may be the treasurer who says, 'We haven't lost it yet, but it's getting real spooky here.' And we have a meeting of the minds, adjust our strategy, and move on. My objective is to obviate risk. If I start failing, and the performance model shows one strategy is costing more than another to obviate risk, then we would have our discussions.

Everyone knows that traders go sour: one week they talk to the gods, and another week God only knows who they are talking to, but you wish they would stop. We don't have that kind of program here—and given the day-to-day performance evaluation and no-surprise attitude we've developed, it's hard for me to envision that scenario playing itself out. If it did play itself out, someone wasn't communicating. There is no reason to lose money every day and walk in on day 30 and say, 'I lost $3 million, try to do better next month.' That doesn't play well here.

In other words, because they hold you responsible for your aggression, that also means greater supervision.

Wells: Yes, daily supervision. You can call it supervision or you can call it interaction. Interaction in risk management is very important because no one individual has the right answer all the time. That interaction allows ideas to bounce around. By bouncing those ideas off one another, you get a nice even strategy that's flexible.

You have talked to lone wolves, I'm sure, and those people are very opinionated. They're convinced that they're right, but the only problem is they're wrong. But they refuse to accept it. That's the worst disease a risk manager can contract. The second worse is the group overall falling susceptible to the same program.

I think that not falling into that trap is the most difficult thing in risk managment—that is, dealing with just-knowing-you're-right disease. If I knew the dollar was going to 1.72 within the next 48 hours, that would suggest that I do something. If I think it might, then I'm also implicitly saying that I don't know that it will, that it's a possibility it might not. That suggests a completely different strategy in my mind—a more prudent strategy.

Are there strategies that you have specifically customized to hedge Compaq's exposures?

Wells: No. We've never built customized strategies, that we've worked out to the nth degree. We try to do a building block approach, identifying what the problems are, what the possible solutions are, and work from there.

Exposures that I'm confronted with—it's kind of a continuous flow process. I don't have large discrete exposures coming at me since we are in the PC business. We are not a $3 billion company by selling three boxes a month. With this continuous flow coming at me, developing a customized approach is kind of hard to envision.

Some people would say that you can, but we've chosen to adopt the building block approach. When you say customized, I also infer inflexible. By taking a building block approach, I can change my tactics. If you so customize something, and something doesn't work out right, you better have plan B. We try to avoid customization at all costs.

Let me give you an example of how that works: Let's assume that the company introduces product Z. There are many inputs, so I customize them to fit particular contracts and exposures associated with that product. But supplier Z can't come up with the goods, so we must take a different appraoch. Supplier A may have a different approach to the problem technically and financially, so now the customized program is in shambles. It's as simple as that. Therefore, I'm much better hedging using the building blocks so that, if supplier Z drops out and is replaced by A, I can adjust my program and move on. That's happened in the past.

In other words, you anticpate an exposure of X million yen, but not necessarily from a specific supplier?

Wells: Right. Assuming the product will go through. That's another thing I've got to consider—the technology. If I were to react to everyone, I'd go crazy. What I'm trying to say is that I must anticipate the unexpected to ensure that my flexibility can be guaranteed.

Life changes in the technology business, and the only certainty is nothing stays the same. So we try to adapt, to keep all of our options open. Don't ever get too carried away with customization, because you may end up with a hedge that isn't working anymore. Then what do you do?

Do your activities benefit Compaq's bottom line?

Wells: No. We are risk averse. What they do is neutralize and smooth out the impact of foreign exchange on the bottom line.

And before you got here, was that also the objective?

Wells: It really evolved. They had already gone through the strong-dollar period. It wasn't that much fun with the dollar at DEM 3.40. To say that it was would be crazy.

Has implementation of a risk management strategy made you more competitive?

Wells: Again, the policy is to neutralize and smooth. Obviously, we are opportunistic when the percentages are in our favor, but overall, the answer is no. That's goes back to my point of being a service organization, not a profit center.

Why do many companies in the computer industry seem to be structured with a more aggressive posture in managing risk?

Wells: I could be wrong, but a lot of us are new and younger companies. We were born with exposures to these risks, as opposed to watching them evolve.

Computer manufacturers have had to deal with risk exposure from day one. Contrast that to another purely domestic company that is suddenly faced with foreign competition, or acquires a foreign business and ends up with the exposures. I've asked myself the same question and that is the only reason I can find.

Perhaps, too, when you're are a young company, a buy-and-hold strategy can get real expensive. And if you haven't got the money to pay for that luxury or indifference, then you have to have plan B—that is, to be more proactive.

Does foreign exchange risk management help you service customers, or give you an edge in competing?

Wells: No. But it helped stabilize earnings. The objective was never to gain a competitive edge through foreign exchange. That goes back to our discussion of strategic issues. Anything that I can do here is fleeting. If you are a $3 billion company, what can I possibly do to guarantee our customers security for the next two years? Nothing. That becomes a strategic issue of how we can better serve our customers. I'm not sure that's a treasury issue or a risk management issue.

8

Eastman Kodak

One of the things that worries me about even talking about this issue is that I look at this as giving us a competitive advantage. And I don't want to give that to anybody else. I agree with the statement that it clearly ought to be a beneficial activity from a shareholder's standpoint to understand this, but how you communicate that, I don't know. You won't find an analyst in a 1,000 that really understands this, and even fewer shareholders.

> — C. Michael Hamilton
> *Treasurer*
> Eastman Kodak

If we say that reality opens up some less precise areas for interpretation and that we aren't very comfortable allowing hedge accounting treatment for those areas, that's kind of a head-in-the-sand approach. Sooner or later, there will have to be an accommodation in this area. The economic problems that companies face have to be addressed, and sometime in the future there will have to be some meeting of the minds between the accounting perspective and the economic perspective.

> — DAVID L. FIEDLER
> *Foreign Exchange Planning Director*
> Eastman Kodak

**Table 8.1   Performance in Review: Eastman Kodak
Income Statement (U.S. Dollars in Millions)**

	1980	1981	1982	1983	1984
+ Sales	$9,734	$10,337	$10,815	$10,170	$10,600
– Cost of Goods Sold	($7,437)	($7,825)	($8,382)	($8,492)	($8,289)
Gross Profit	$2,297	$2,512	$2,433	$1,678	$2,311
Gross Profit %	23.6%	24.3%	22.5%	16.5%	21.8%
–Depreciation	($399)	($454)	($575)	($653)	($760)
–Other Costs	$72	$126	$5	$3	$73
PB1	$1,970	$2,184	$1,863	$1,028	$1,624
–Taxes	($812)	($943)	($706)	($458)	($701)
Taxes %	-41.2%	-43.2%	-37.9%	-44.6%	-43.2%
Net Income	$1,158	$1,240	$1,157	$570	$922
Net Income %	11.9%	12.0%	10.7%	5.6%	8.7%
Working Capital	$2,998	$2,944	$3,143	$3,248	$2,825
Working Capital/Sales %	30.8%	28.5%	29.1%	31.9%	26.7%
Long-term Debt	$208	$208	$489	$630	$612
Long-term Debt/Sales %	2.1%	2.0%	4.5%	6.2%	5.8%
Earnings Per Share	$3.18	$3.40	$3.16	$1.52	$2.54
Cash Flow Per Share	$4.28	$4.63	$4.66	$3.27	$4.81
Average Annual P/E	8.1	9.4	11.0	22.1	12.3

1985	1986	1987	1988	1989	Average	CAGR %
$10,631	$11,550	$13,305	$17,034	$18,398	$12,257	7.3%
($8,664)	($9,332	($10,205)	($12,912)	($14,608)	($9,615)	7.8%
$1,967	$2,218	$3,100	$4,122	$3,790	$2,643	5.7%
18.5%	19.2%	23.3%	24.2%	20.6%	21.4%	-1.5%
($838)	($975)	($995)	($1,183)	($1,326)	($816)	14.3%
($602)	($651)	($112)	($704)	($1,531)	($332)	
$526	$591	$1,994	$2,235	$933	$1,495	-8.0%
($197)	($222)	($809)	($838)	($399)	($609)	-7.6%
-37.4%	-37.5%	-40.6%	-37.5%	-42.8%	-40.6%	0.4%
$330	$370	$1,184	$1,397	$534	$886	-8.3%
3.1%	3.2%	8.9%	8.2%	2.9%	7.5%	-14.5%
$2,352	$2,020	$2,620	$2,834	$2,018	$2,700	-4.3%
22.1%	17.5%	19.7%	16.6%	11.0%	23.4%	-10.8%
$988	$911	$2,212	$7,779	$7,376	$2,141	48.7%
9.3%	7.9%	16.6%	45.7%	40.1%	14.0%	38.5%
$0.97	$1.11	$3.52	$4.31	$1.63	$2.53	-7.2%
$3.45	$3.98	$6.71	$7.96	$5.72	$4.95	3.3%
31.2	35.0	15.7	10.2	28.4	18.3	15.0%

Figure 8.1   Eastman Kodak

Imaging

Photographic Products Group

- Consumer Imaging Division
- Consumer Services Division
- Motion Picture & Television
  Products Division
- Professional Photography
  Division

Chemicals

Eastman Chemical Company

- Chemicals
- Plastics
- Fibers

Health

- Sterling Drug Inc.
- Health Sciences Division
- Clinical Products Division
- Lehn & Fink Products

Information Systems

Commercial Systems Group

*Imaging Information Systems
Group*

Eastman Kodak:
Responding to Foreign Competition

In the mind of David L. Fiedler, foreign exchange planning director for Eastman Kodak in Rochester, N.Y., the reason to develop a strategic currency risk management hedging program became most apparent from 1980 to 1985. During that time, Kodak had watched global market share and profitability in the imaging sector of its business come under increasing pressure from competitors. In particular, the second largest consumer film producer, Fuji Photo,

**Figure 8.2   Performance in Review:
Eastman Kodak (1980–1989)**

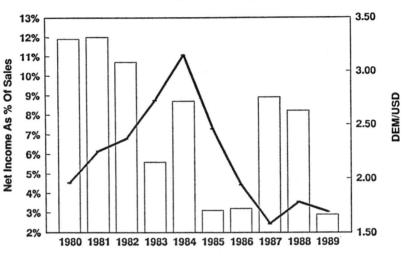

was benefitting from the yen/dollar exchange rate. With a weak yen, Fuji's largely yen-denominated cost of production was less than Kodak's dollar-denominated production. This limited Kodak's options in protecting its sizable U.S. market share and positioning in other overseas markets.

The year 1985, in particular, was a disappointing year for Kodak largely because of the impact that foreign currency risk was having on the overall competitiveness of the corporation. While overall sales advanced in real terms at a reasonable rate, in dollars terms they amounted to $10.6 billion, only $31 million more than the previous year. For nearly five years, Kodak's results had been depressed by the relentless surge of the U.S. dollar. This situation dramatized how competitive currency exposures arise from the denomination of a company's costs, the denomination of the competition's costs, and what impact this can have on the firm's ability to maintain profit margins.

Kodak wasn't completely ignoring the problem. Like many multi-national corporations, it had developed a profit-driven foreign exchange operation to manage its foreign exchange exposures. This group traded for profit against natural positions created by its global business activities. The interesting twist was that, while such operations were generating their share of profits, they were still not able to stop a loss of market share in the U.S. film business.

How bad was the damage? Fiedler, a native of Minneapolis, Minn., who has worked for Kodak since 1969, likes to refer to the company's 1985 annual report, in which then chairman and CEO Colby H. Chandler estimated that Kodak's earnings would have been increased "by an aggregate of about $3.5 billion." That is, if the exchange rates of 1980 had prevailed, instead of the surge of the U.S. dollar by over 40 percent during that time period.

In 1984, Fiedler was training to become part of Eastman Kodak's profit-driven foreign exchange operation, trading foreign exchange on the trading desk of Bank of America in New York as a Kodak employee. This work was a natural progression from his adminstrative and systems responsibilities with Kodak from 1969 to 1979 and his work as director of cash management from 1979 to Fall 1984. It was a corporate sabbatical of sorts that he intended to put to good use. While trading and researching the foreign exchange markets, he collected an idea that strategic currency risk must also be managed, if he was going to help maintain the company's competitive position in the U.S. market and also globally.

To recommend how strategic currency risk might be managed by blending foreign exchange expertise with the product-related expertise of operating units, Fiedler went to the highest levels of management. He sought approval for currency hedging programs that would not only deal with shorter-term transactional exposures, but also with long-term competitive exposures. Both Fiedler and Eastman Kodak Treasurer C. Michael Hamilton credit the company's senior management for recognition of this problem and taking action against it, and also Abraham George, President of Multinational Computer Models in New Jersey, who helped Fiedler develop a strategic framework from which to execute a competitive foreign exchange strategy.

"I do believe that Colby [H. Chandler, then chairman and CEO] was very astute in these matters," says Hamilton. "There was a clear recognition of the impact of foreign exchange on earnings because of the overvalued dollar in the early 80s. Colby's feeling was, to the extent that we were a dollar-cost company, and the dollar was overvalued, that it prevented us from competing effectively, and restricted out ability to raise prices without potentially eroding market share."

Kodak has since accepted the challenge of global competition in the 1990s, realigning and restructuring its business to focus on four strategic businesses—imaging, chemicals, health and information systems. At its strategic center is imaging, from which chemicals, health, and information form natural growth lines. But from the very start, the manufacturing of film, as well as its processing, required chemicals and remains a key business for the company.

- **Imaging:** For amateur photography, Kodak supplies cameras, projectors, films, processing services, photographic papers, batteries, and chemicals. Kodak products for nonamateur photography include films, photographic papers, photographic plates, chemicals, processing equipment and audiovisual equipment. Nonamateur products serve professional photofinishers and photographers and customers in motion picture, television, audiovisual, industry, financial, commercial and government markets. Kodak's imaging products and services compete with similar products and services of other competitors such as Fuji. Competition in traditional imaging markets is strong throughout the world. Many large and small companies offer similar products and services that compete with Kodak's business. Sales for this segment of Kodak's business totaled $6.9 billion in 1989. Silver, the price of which has fluctuated significantly in recent years, is one of the essential materials in photographic film and

Figure 8.3   Silver Price Indices in U.S. Dollar & Japanese Yen terms (1973–1990)

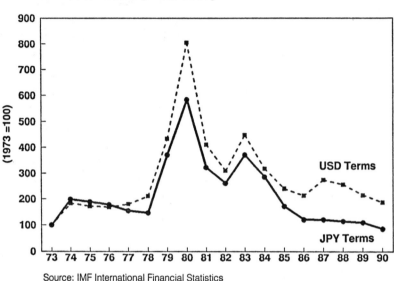

Source: IMF International Financial Statistics

paper manufacture (See Figure 8.3). Kodak's imaging manufacturing facililties are located in the U.S., Australia, Brazil, Canada, the United Kingdom, France, Germany, and Mexico.

• **Information systems.** This segment of Kodak consists of businesses that serve the imaging and information needs of business, industry, and government. Products in this segment are used to capture, store, process, and display images and information in a variety of forms. Kodak purchases, manufactures, and markets various components of information systems and provides service agreements to support these products. Information systems products include graphic arts film, microfilm products, magnetic media, applications software, copiers, printers, and other business equipment. These products serve the needs of customers in the commercial printing and publishing, office automation and government markets. Products within this division also face strong competition from competitors such as Xerox and Pitney Bowes. Electronic components represent significant portion of the overall costs in building equipment, and the sources for which are from Japan and other countries, creating both transactional and strategic foreign exchange risks for Kodak. The 1989 sales for this segment were $4.2 billion. These products are manufactured primarily in the U.S., with facilities also in Ireland, Germany, Brazil, and Mexico.

- **Chemicals.** Kodak's chemical products are principally classified into four groups: olefin, acetyl, polyester, and speciality and fine chemical products. Polyesters are marketed for a variety of plastic uses, including bottles for beverages. Specialty and fine chemical products include photographic chemicals sold to the Kodak imaging segment, health and nutrition products, and high-technology organic chemicals, including complex intermediates sold to pharmaceutical companies for further conversion to prescription drugs. These products compete with similar products of other large chemical manufacturers. Sales totaled $3.5 billion in 1989 and production occurs in various parts of the U.S. and the United Kingdom.

- **Health.** Kodak manufactures and markets pharmaceutical products including prescription medicines andthose made specifically for use in hospitals, non-prescription health products, and hospital supplies such as X-ray film, screens, cassettes, process, and chemicals for radiography market, as wells as blood analysis equipment and consumables such as disinfectants, all purpose cleaners, floor-care products, rodenticides, wood stains, concrete and wood protectors, deodorants, and hair-care products. In this area, many of Kodak's competitors are engaged in

119

Figure 8.4   Lufthansa DEM Hedge Alternatives

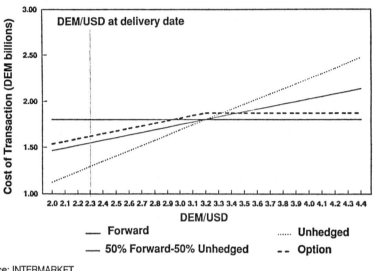

Source: INTERMARKET

research and development of products that could constitute additional competition. Sales totaled $4.0 billion in 1989. Manufacturing is done in the U.S., Puerto Rico, Canada, the United Kingdom, and France.

To make all of these businesses more competitive globally, Fiedler communicates with senior management and leaders of these operating divisions to identify the competition, their sourcing and pricing strategies, and how sensitive Kodak's market share may be to changes in currency exchange rates. In many cases, structural solutions may be pursued, such as sourcing materials from a different company. In still other cases, Kodak may make use of the many financial instruments available to hedge currency risk—including forwards, swaps, and options.

According to Fiedler, options are the financial tool that specifically makes the most sense in managing strategic currency risks. As proof,

Table 8.2   Lufthansa Hedge Alternatives

DEM/USD	Time 0 Principal in DEM	Unhedged Principal in DEM	50% Forward/ 50% Unhedged Strategy	Option Strategy	Option Cost
2.0	1.80	1.13	1.46	1.53	0.07
2.1	1.80	1.18	1.49	1.56	0.07
2.2	1.80	1.24	1.52	1.59	0.07
2.3	1.80	1.29	1.55	1.62	0.07
2.4	1.80	1.35	1.58	1.65	0.07
2.5	1.80	1.41	1.60	1.68	0.07
2.6	1.80	1.46	1.63	1.70	0.07
2.7	1.80	1.52	1.66	1.73	0.07
2.8	1.80	1.58	1.69	1.76	0.07
2.9	1.80	1.63	1.72	1.79	0.07
3.0	1.80	1.69	1.74	1.82	0.07
3.1	1.80	1.74	1.77	1.84	0.07
3.2	1.80	1.80	1.80	1.87	0.07
3.3	1.80	1.86	1.83	1.87	0.07
3.4	1.80	1.91	1.86	1.87	0.07
3.5	1.80	1.97	1.88	1.87	0.07
3.6	1.80	2.02	1.91	1.87	0.07
3.7	1.80	2.08	1.94	1.87	0.07
3.8	1.80	2.14	1.97	1.87	0.07
3.9	1.80	2.19	2.00	1.87	0.07
4.0	1.80	2.25	2.02	1.87	0.07
4.1	1.80	2.31	2.05	1.87	0.07
4.2	1.80	2.36	2.08	1.87	0.07
4.3	1.80	2.42	2.11	1.87	0.07
4.4	1.80	2.47	2.14	1.87	0.07

Source: INTERMARKET

he is always quick to allude to the experience of Lufthansa Airlines. Lufthansa purchased 20 Boeing 737s in 1985, just as the dollar was peaking in February 1985. The airline locked in half of this $500 million purchase with forwards at an exchange rate of DM 3.20, avoiding any currency risk on half its exposure and leaving the other half unhedged. As the dollar weakened, Lufthansa thus paid an opportunity cost of $73 million by locking in the stronger dollar rate on 50 percent of this exposure. Heinz Ruhnau, chairman of the executive board at Lufthansa German Airlines, was held responsible for the transaction, and the airline's supervisory board considered not renewing his contract.[1] "Lufthansa's intent to manage the risk associated with purchasing these aircraft was a good one," says Fiedler. "Unfortunately, it was an all-or-nothing strategy that was pursued. Options are a much more flexible way to layer in a strategy, with the only cost being the upfront premium that you pay. Options can eliminate the risk of losing such opportunities, whether you are managing a tactical or strategic exposure." (See Figure 8.4, Table 8.2).

In this interview, Fiedler and Hamilton explain why economic risk is a problem that all U.S. corporations must address; how U.S. accounting convention has not kept up with accurately mirroring the "economic reality" U.S. multinational corporations face as they compete globally; and how Kodak defines, monitors, and addresses the currency risk it faces.

Interview:
C. Michael Hamilton and
David L. Fiedler

From a practitioner's point of view, what are some of the largest U.S. companies that have strategic currency risks to address?

Fiedler: GM is certainly one today because it has the very real problem of Japanese auto manufacturers building plants in the U.S.

and also importing cars into the U.S. In fact, all U.S. car companies had strategic problems when the Japanese were simply importing into the U.S. in the early '80s, although they now face a broader range of economic problems.

Another corporation mentioned a lot is Caterpillar, which faces the same problem in competing against Komatsu in the U.S. market as we face against some of our global competitors. But the basic point that every corporation should understand about economic risk is that it doesn't matter where you are competing. Whether you're competing against a foreign company in your home market, or offshore against a foreign domestic company in its home country, or offshore against a foreign competitor in a third country—it doesn't really matter. There will be an economic impact on your competitive position as the exchange rates of the particular countries move. Obviously your home currency, the currency of your competitor, and the currency where you are competing are all going to be factors. The currencies where you and your competitors are manufacturing will also be an issue.

But you may say—"Wait a minute. Foreign competition and foreign currencies have always been an issue, so why are they more important now?" The answer is what has happened to volatility in the capital markets since the advent of floating exchange rates. Volatility has increased the probability that currency exchange rates can help or hurt the competitive postures of companies more dramatically.

Some other issues influence why this has become a major problem as well. If you look at it from a U.S. perspective, the comparitive dominance to U.S. industry in the world economy was at its peak right after World War II. The rest of the industrial world was essentially decimated, and this gave us a very large piece of world GNP. I believe it was as high as 50 percent right after the war. The last time I saw a calculation, it was something like 23 percent of world GNP, down about 50 percent from what it had been 25 or so years earlier. What's important, I think, as we look at the position of the U.S. in the world economy and where it's likely to be in the future, is that it will have a much smaller piece of world GNP than it had during than post-war period.

In the '50s and '60s, the U.S. was unbelievably successful from an economic standpoint. But as you look forward, it's not that the U.S. won't necessarily thrive and do well economically, but its percentage of world GNP will continue to decrease as other parts of the world like the Pacific Rim, Latin America, and Eastern Europe begin to industrialize. As a result, the odds of your competition being foreign competition will be higher and higher as well. So, earlier, the chances of your competition being another U.S. company were very good. Combine that with much lower volatility in a period of fixed exchange rates, and the problem didn't seem that big, although the problem was always there. At one time in our history, it just didn't make much difference. Now, it has increased in importance and is not likely to go away.

What are some real-life examples of industries in which there were no foreign competitors, which now have a significant number?

Fiedler: We have already mentioned one—the auto industry. Another classic example is the U.S. steel industry. It has virtually disappeared from the U.S. over the last couple of decades. They are the two best examples I can think of. But, really, you can almost flip around that question and say: "It's hard to find an industry today that isn't seriously affected." Obviously, service industries will not tend to be affected in the same way. But in the manufacturing sector, it's hard to find companies that are not increasingly being impacted by foreign competition.

Closer to home, we have been significantly impacted. The further you go back in time, the less competition we had in the photographic piece of our business. And, although it is no longer the sum total of what Kodak is all about, it's still significant to us.

Today, we have some very serious competitors in the photographic area. Fuji Photo is clearly the number one competitor in the photographic industry. We are competing with them very seriously in the U.S. market, although we still have a very dominant share of market

124

in the U.S. And we are competing with competitors such as Fuji all around the world.

Hamilton: And we are also more aware of the impact that strategic currency risks can have on our business results and how managing such risk can actually help us from a business standpoint. Others may be less so. The great example of this: U.S. companies that still don't think they have any foreign exchange exposure because they manufacture in dollars and sell in dollars. In fact, if they have competition from anyone who does those things outside the U.S., they have a foreign exchange problem. Saying that you make widgets here and sell them here doesn't mean that you don't have a problem.

Fiedler: Right. It can also mean that you can go bankrupt here, if you don't pay attention to this problem.

Are we ever going to see more "stable" exchange rates? Before you endorse economic hedging, I suppose you have to believe this is an unlikely reality to be played out in the future?

Fiedler: We have come to an age where the world powers have appeared to recognize the need for coordination. Some say that will be a trend and volatility ought to be going down. In the Plaza accord period, that coordination didn't really happen. All of the rhetoric was cooperation, but the reality was that it was convenient at that point in time because economic situations in individual countries happened to support common economic policy.

Also, if you look back, that was where the market was going anyway. The market didn't peak in September 1985; it peaked in February 1985. It was already going down by the time the G-7 got involved in the party. Volatility in foreign exchange markets will only begin to disappear when all of the countries involved have their domestic houses in order. That is when you will find equilibrium.

If you want to look at problems that Japan is having today, it is partially because they cooperated back in 1985 to help the U.S. They lowered Japanese interest rates and those unrealistically low interest rates also unrealistically inflated stock and real estate markets in Japan.

But to answer your question without some rhetoric of my own, it's conceivable that we will reach a time in the future that volatility will not be as high as it is today. It will be more likely, however, that volatility will increase for some time into the future, I believe.

Admittedly, volatility isn't a one-way street. It will come down at some point. But will it return to a period of low volatility like we had when exchange markets were fixed in the Bretton Woods Era? I don't think so. Most academics have concluded that we can't go home. We couldn't fix rates again today if we wanted. The world is becoming increasingly less fettered by control, whether it is central banks or regulation of domestic capital markets, as we move more and more towards a truly global economy. The only thing that will reduce volatility is economic discipline.

Dave, when did you develop the policy to manage strategic currency risk?

Fiedler: In May 1988.

Mike, what has your role been in this process and your attitude about what strategic hedging can do for Kodak?

Hamilton: I'm not going to be able to go back too much before May 1988, because I became treasurer in January 1988. Prior to that, I was part of a different financial operation, but let me give you my impressions. Prior to Dave's involvement in foreign exchange, the company was simply a trading operation. It was trying to manage what was perceived to be the foreign exchange risk on the balance sheet and was designed to give us a reading on the market. The policy of hedging Kodak's exposure was very short term.

After Dave arrived and after selling Kodak management in May 1988, what culminated was a strategic policy and program. Management recognized that managing Kodak's foreign exchange exposure was a much larger problem and issue than simply what appeared each quarter on the balance sheet. What has developed on that basis over time—with Dave leading the charge—is our senior management is beginning to see they need to really look at the foreign exchange exposure at a much longer term level. Independent of the accounting records, they are looking at our cash flow exposure. Therefore, our efforts in the foreign exchange area have dramatically shifted. We still have a trading operation for market intelligence purposes, but we are much more concerned with the longer term strategic exposures.

If we can manage that better than our competition, my feeling is it gives us a competitive advantage. It all boils down to that statement. For me, to the extent that we can use our financial acumen within Kodak to give the company a competitive advantage from a business standpoint, that's what we should be doing.

Can you talk about your management of interest rate risk? The acquisition of Sterling Drug clearly makes this a strategic issue as well, doesn't it?

Hamilton: It does. We are trying to do similar things with our interest rate exposure, but that has just started. We have managed strategic foreign exchange exposures longer than anything else. With the acquisition of Sterling Drug, we took on an additional $5 billion in debt. That acquisition basically doubled the amount of debt that we have, and therefore the management of interest rate risk became a real issue.

We bought Sterling Drug with a consortium of 23 banks and used a bank revolver. We then paid all of the banks back by refinancing with commercial paper and fixed rate debt over several months after the acquisition. As a result, we've tried to make judgments as to when to fix some of the floating rate debt, so we've had some fairly large U.S. issues.

At the time, it was less expensive to issue in the U.S. than anywhere else, and since the acquisiton, we now have fixed about 60 percent of our debt. For the 40 percent that is floating, we have used caps at times to put a ceiling on our exposure to higher rates. But primarily, we have tried to manage this risk by fixing an all-in cost that we believe over time will be attractive.

Prior to Sterling, there was very little active interest rate risk management at Kodak because we had little or no debt. Since then, we have tried to look at future cash flows, how they correlate with interest rate movements, and reach some conclusions about the interrelationship between interest rate levels and cash flows. That's basically what we've tried to do—look at our cash flows and try to make some prudent judgments about rates.

We are not trying to guess rates, but rather to look back over time and say, "We are not sure what will happen in the future. But if we have all-in costs of a certain amount for longer periods of time, we would feel good about going ahead and fixing that." As a result, we have gone from 60 percent floating to 40 percent floating since the acquisition.

Tell me about your strategic currency risk management program and how you started to implement it.

Fiedler: We actually entered into some strategic transactions that predated when the policy was in place, just because we felt from an opportunity standpoint that there were some things that we didn't want to miss—particularly the weaker dollar. In a sense, those transactions were pilots, but they preceded approval of the policy itself.

So you dipped your toes first, Mike, so to speak?

Hamilton: Yes. Our decision is reflective of the fact that when you are dealing with an exposure that can be very very large, and have a significant financial impact on the company, a lot of U.S. companies are not just going to just jump on a new idea lock, stock, and barrel. And that included us. Without having some kind of experience as to how it works and what it means, we've had a gestation period of several years. Since then, we've decided that the program really is something we want to go forward with.

So where are you in this evolutionary process of managing strategic risks?

Fiedler: If you view our program as evolving, I think we are still educating and injecting a level of understanding and awareness into all of our operations. I think that will go on for several years into the future before everything is in place.

It must not have been easy to get your initial strategic programs rolling. You must have faced roadblocks.

Hamilton: Our experience was that we started out with these kinds of programs at the very highest level within the corporation—that is, the CEO and the President. Once you've gained support and got the process going, you have support to go into the organization at a slightly lower level, perhaps at the operating unit level. It may be that you always must start at the top, at least in the beginning. That's what we did.

So what you're telling me is that those examples would be pilot programs, without formal approval from operating units? That you kept the CEO and President well informed, were successful, and that created some room for future strategic risk programs later on?

Hamilton: Right.

Fiedler: I might add that I'm not sure that when we did those that it was as much an implementation strategy because of the size of the program. They were the decision makers, so there was a little serendipity in there too. But it's true that it had a big impact on the future success of the program.

So how do you define economic risk exposure and go about managing it?

Fiedler: What we have done is operationally divide the exposure into two pieces—tactical exposure and strategic exposure. The tactical piece includes worldwide transaction accounting exposure. It will also include other things of a relatively short-term nature—say, a year or less—that are not currently recorded under accounting convention. That would include dividends, royalties, various technical fees, and those types of exposures.

With strategic exposures, the common denominator is that they are all exposures currently unrecorded under current accounting conventions. Generally speaking, such exposures will have a considerably longer term time horizon.

From what I've said, you could assume that tactical is just short term, but that's just one piece of it. It could be very long term as well. If you had a ten-year borrowing in a foreign currency on your books, it's a transactional accounting exposure. As such it's going to be a tactical exposure. So it's not quite correct to say it's just a time break that defines these two types of exposures. But it's true that tactical tends to be the short-term piece of the problem, both recorded and unrecorded. Likewise, strategic tends to be the longer term piece of the problem.

With the tactical piece, we are currently centralizing that exposure on a worldwide basis. It's managed on a consolidated basis from Rochester. What that means for the subsidiaries is that on a periodic basis, once a quarter, they provide us with their balance sheets in actual currency of exposure. So it's not a result that's translated into their local currency or into dollars, but rather in the actual currencies of exposure. We then consolidate those exposures worldwide and manage the net exposure.

You have to do a couple of things to consolidate so that you have apples and apples. Specifically, you need to look at where the exposures are coming from in terms of the effective tax rate of the jurisdictions involved and to decompose the exposures into their dollar component pieces. For example, if we had a Deutschemark receivable on our U.K. books, that's really long marks versus short sterling. But we could think of it as long marks-short dollars, long dollars-short sterling, where the dollar amounts are equal but opposite in sign. As a result, they cancel out. By breaking them into their dollar component pieces, we end up with all dollar-something exposures. If you are looking at them on an after-tax basis, you really do have apples and apples. We can net those worldwide and manage that net result.

On what basis do you manage the net result?

Fiedler: Once we have identified our exposures in dollar terms, we manage these exposures against a 100 percent hedged standard. Some companies have an objective of being 100 percent hedged. If they know they have an exposure, their objective is to have it fully hedged. In contrast, our *standard* is what would have happened if we had hedged 100 percent of the exposure, and our *objective* is to add value against that standard.

From the standpoint of the operating units, this means they are less involved in the tactical problem today than they were in the past. On the surface, that could sound like the wrong direction, but there is a specific reason for that.

For one, we firmly believe that in terms of concentration of expertise and transaction costs, this is clearly the most efficient way to manage the problem. For example, suppose you had two subsidiaries that had exactly opposite exposures, so your net exposure is actually zero. If you said one is long, one is short, at the same tax rates, in the same counter currency of the exposure, they are naturally hedged, one against the other. If they were both individually hedging the transaction, you are going to incur transaction costs on both sides. And if they were both fully hedged, they would be doing the exact opposite: one would be buying while the other is selling. You could also end up with situations where both parties are doing exactly the wrong thing, and you magnify the exposure as a result. So, on the tactical side, there are some real payoffs by consolidating and managing the net result centrally.

Is it possible for a corporation to effectively manage its financial risks if operating managers throughout the business are not quite aware of what's going on in the financial markets? I would have to say, no, it probably isn't. The financial decisions are ultimately totally integrated with other operating decisions, and if you try to deal with them independently, you're going to get suboptimal answers, or perhaps just wrong answers. But what we would argue is that the problem operating management should be worrying about is not the day-to-day kind of problem, anyway, which is the essence of the tactical problem. Their concern should really be what's happening from a longer term perspective in various capital markets and that's what we want operating management to focus on—to clearly see. By taking the tactical problem off their plate, they can focus on the strategic aspects of the problem. And that's where the real impact of foreign exchange risk management can be over a period of time.

Switching to the strategic piece, it's very difficult to look at a strategic problem and deal with the financial aspects of it in isolation. In terms of the whole range of alternatives that operating management have in dealing with various strategic problems, financial transactions are only one piece of that total picture.

And many corporations have other operational alternatives that may be more viable at any given point in time.

Fiedler: Right. Those interrelationships—where do you locate a plant versus purely financial transactions—are worth thinking about. At the point you've defined what your economic problem is, the reality is there are going to be a broad range of solutions out there. If you divide up the problem, you will find that there are subsets of alternatives that are better suited for various pieces of your economic exposure. It doesn't make sense not to look at all of the possible solutions and try to select out the optimal one. Sometimes that may be a financial market transaction; other times it may not be. And the more structural the problem, the more likely the ultimate answer will be something other than a financial market transaction.

What percent of your solutions are financial versus structural?

Fiedler: That's a question I can't honestly give you a good answer to, because we are in a state of evolution on that issue.

I mentioned that the strategic policy was approved in May 1988. But the first piece of the problem that we tackled in terms of implementation was the tactical piece—not because we viewed it as the most important piece, but because it's the most visible piece. It needed to be done first from a practical perspective. The heart of the tactical problem is what's going to be reported in earnings each quarter and so forth, so from necessity we felt that we needed to address that first. That's what we did for the balance of 1988, and that piece of it has pretty much been in place since that time.

As time has passed, we have concentrated more and more on pushing out the time continuum toward the increasingly strategic aspects of the problem. We have done a fair amount of work in the whole area of foreign sourcing, for example. And we are doing work on the competitive aspects of the problem as well. But although we have done a number of things, some of which have been quite large, I would still characterize where we are in the implementation process as being in the early stages.

One of the important things we're doing is spending a lot of time building communication links with the operating units—the people who are the fundamental creators and owners of strategic exposure. That takes a fair amount of time. As we do that, we are getting an increasingly better understanding of the problems of operating units. Operating units, in turn, are getting a better understanding of how the economic problem is related to what they do. You need to have a pretty good foundation built up in both directions in order to manage economic risk successfuly.

Maybe one way of answering your question—in a way that is not numerical or quantitative—is to say that over time, we should see an increasing number of solutions to strategic problems that are not financial transactions.

What about taking a cash flow perspective on economic risk when your business is widgets? It's true that some of your company's products are probably more sensitive to competition than others, isn't it? Doesn't economic risk management need to be done on a product-by-product basis?

Fiedler: Yes, that's really the right way to look at it—if you think of a corporation as a portfolio of investments, and individual products or groups of products as investments in the portfolio.

However, that's a departure from how many academics perceive the problem. What I'm talking about is the notion that if you do some sort of macro calculation of your economic exposure to various types of risk—currencies, interest rates, and commodity risk as well—you may not come up with a useful solution. Such an analysis will conclude that you need a macro hedge to deal with that problem. But how do you know, if you've taken this snapshot of some point in time or taken a look at the last 10 years of history, that it's in any way representative of the future? Your attempt to look at the problem and address it has to be forward looking, not backward looking. In addition, there may be many pieces of your complete portfolio that really aren't exposed. As rates move, cash flows for those investments might not change over time. If that's the case, my feeling is that we ought to back that out of the equation and focus on where our problem really is.

So it's more appropriate to say that a strategic risk management program on a product basis is something you are working towards, not something that is complete?

Fiedler: Yes, I think that's a better way to put it. We approved a new foreign exchange policy two years ago and have been systemati-cally implementing that policy. Various pieces are in different stages of implementation. Some have been complete for some period of time. With others we've done things, but haven't necessarily done every-thing that we can do. And in fact, it's a dynamic problem, so there will always be things to do.

But that's the way you must look at it. If I look at my business as an $18 billion portfolio, to look at it as one business is incorrect. It's a portfolio of many different businesses. If you look at it the impact of financial risks, you need to look at what is having an impact and where it is having an impact, and what you can do about it.

Let me ask a question for investors and shareholders. Is there any industry in which you shouldn't be managing economic risk? Isn't a shareholder who is investing in an oil company doing it because he is in some way speculating on the price of oil? Does the justification for managing economic risk hold for every industry, and every company?

Fiedler: There are different ways of coming at that. If it doesn't make any difference to your cash flows if you manage risk, then perhaps it does not make sense to incur the expense related to hedg-ing. The Modigliani/Miller proposition, I suppose, in some way as-serts that. But to me, that's the basic question to ask—as a result of managing economic exposure, can you improve the return to the shareholder? As far as I'm concerned, that's the justification for man-aging the problem.

There's kind of a separate issue that you raised—what is it that the shareholder is after? A matter of practical reality, the bulk of U.S. corporations have dollar-based shareholders. And you can argue that a foreign investor invests in Kodak because he wants to be exposed to dollars. Therefore, to the extent that you implement a hedging action focused on maximizing the dollar value of the corporation, that's consistent with the intention of the investor as well. That may or may not be true.

But somewhere along the line there has to be some sort of stake in the ground. I think, for most U.S. corporations, the basic question ought to be: if we do something about various forms of financial risk, will it increase shareholder value? And if the conclusion is yes, which is a conclusion that we've come to, that's justification for doing it.

Does a company with raw material requirements like yours also look at those costs as cash flow in some sense?

Fiedler: Absolutely. That's the common denominator. This is probably a good point to refer back to the SEC's comments last summer (in 1989), because some very specific things were said. For one, the SEC said if a transaction can't be designated under accounting rules as a hedge, then you have to mark it to market. If it can be designated as a hedge, then you may be able to get hedge accounting treatment. In other words, you can defer the economic result of the hedge until you recognize what was hedged. So all we are really talking about is accounting symmetry: *when* you report the result of the hedge and the result of what was hedged.

The SEC also said that if you enter into a transaction to hedge net income, you can't get hedge accounting treatment on that transaction because net income is not a transaction. Suppose you have a German subsidiary and are forecasting at the beginnng of the year that it will be producing net income of DM200. And also assume that at the beginning of the year the exchange rate is 2 marks per dollar—the forecast result would be net income of $100.

But let's suppose that at the end of the year, the rate has gone to 1:1. Ignoring that income is calculated using an average exchange rate for the interval, the translated value of that DM200 at 1:1 is $200. Income went up by $100. So the question is—what is the true cash flow impact to the corporation?

Let's look at two possibilities. The income of DM200 could be reinvested in Germany—in a new plant and equipment, that is—to help run that business. In that case, there hasn't actually been any conversion of currency from DM to dollars. You are going to grow a business that will produce future DM cashflows, but what matters is what the value of those cash flows will be when they are actually remitted to the parent company.

But now let's consider that, instead, you are going to take the DM200 and remit it to the parent as a dividend. Now there is a cash flow. That DM income is converted to dollars. If the exchange rate is 2:1, it's $100; if it's 1:1, its $200. That's a real cash flow effect.

At the EITF meeting that's what the SEC was saying—"Look, the fact that a foreign operation generates net income doesn't mean there is any economic event there"—and they are in fact right about that.

There are ways of dealing with that. For one, net income is composed of transactions. If we have net income of DM200— revenues of DM400 and costs of DM200—you may be able to get hedge accounting treatment on the underlying transactions. But there's another part to that problem—where will there be actual cash flows? We would argue that should be our focus. Net income of DM200 is not very material to the exposure problem if there is not going to be a remittance to the parent company. If there is, that's what we should focus on.

There are a lot of U.S. corporations that will talk about addressing the economic problem, and what they mean by that is they have entered into transactions to hedge net income. So obviously when the SEC said that's not a hedgeable transaction, that was really a problem for those companies.

But if your emphasis is on cash flows, the SEC comment really isn't a problem. Hedging net income isn't getting at the root of the economic problem. But behind that, there may be real economic problems, so I'm also saying that I don't completely agree with the SEC's depiction of the problem. In fact, the SEC is still looking at things in accounting terms. And that's where we get those kinds of differences of opinion.

Let's go one step further with another example: imagine a fictitious U.S. corporation that is totally domestic. It manufactures everything that it makes in the U.S., sources all of its raw materials in the U.S., finances itself in dollars, sells everything it makes in the U.S.. It's totally domestic. If we look at its financials and ask if it has exchange risk, the answer would be that, "No, it doesn't." If you look at the accounting perception of the problem, there is no actual exchange risk because it does everything in dollars.

But let's add one more assumption: this fictitious U.S. company has a major foreign competitor in the U.S. market. It's not selling offshore, but it has a foreign competitor selling in the U.S. At that point, it becomes intuitively clear that the company has an economic problem. As the dollar falls, versus the currency of its competitor, the U.S. company will be more competitive against that competitor. As the dollar rises, it will become less competitive. This is an economic problem that will affect the future cash flows of the hypothetical corporation. Most likely, the impact will be felt in terms of market share and margin.

The problem, under accounting conventions, is that we don't record a lost sale as an exposure. We just record what did happen, not what

Figure 8.5   Relationships of Various Types of Exposures

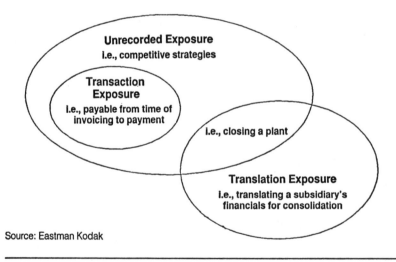

Source: Eastman Kodak

138

could have happened. It's that opportunity effect that's our focus, because it's a real economic problem. The point we are consistently making is, if exchange rate movements will affect our future cash flows, that's material to us, that's of interest to us. That's the focus of the economic problem and the solutions we design to address it.

So that's what this graphic is saying (See Figure 8.5). The economic problem (or shaded area) is going to include a piece of the accounting problem, but it's going to include a lot of other things that, under accounting convention, don't happen to be currently recorded or reported but are going to affect cash flows. At this point, the division between the accounting perception of the problem and the economic perception of the problem gets wider and wider.

In talking with the SEC and FASB, I also found out that one of the deals that caused them concern was Walt Disney's hedge of Disneyland in Tokyo, a 15- or 16-year "hedge." They were saying, there may be economic exposure, but where do we put that stake on how far out you can hedge? Is it three years? If three years is OK, is it five years? 10 years? How about 20?

Fiedler: That's what really bothers the accounting profession: to the extent you allow people to get hedge treatment on things that fall outside the current accounting definition of the problem, you are in a sense opening Pandora's box. Because now, if you are going to hedge against future risk—risk that we haven't recognized under current accounting convention—where do you stop? I can be a little sympathetic to that. But the problem is, that's reality.

If we say that reality opens up some less precise areas for interpretation and that we aren't very comfortable allowing hedge accounting treatment for those areas, that's kind of a head-in-the-sand approach. Sooner or later, there will have to be an accommodation in this area. The economic problems that companies face have to be addressed, and sometime in the future there will have to be some meeting of the minds between the accounting perspective and the economic perspective.

What's to prevent a company doing a hedge for three years, if the market goes from 260 to 250, from reporting those gains in a shorter time period to manipulate the situation?

Fiedler: I don't know if that is so serious a problem. Even under current accounting rules if you hedge something that is not a current transaction, you have to designate what you are hedging. So you are declaring yourself.

If I were an accountant, my concern would be—what's to prevent a company from entering into purely speculative activity by just defining something that isn't a current event, or transaction, and saying that's what they are hedging? All they want to do is buy dollars because they think the dollar is going up, or vice versa.

What would be an example of that?

Fiedler: Well, suppose you have a foreign competitor and you're hurt when the dollar rises. You want to hedge against that—to buy dollars. But the only time you want to buy is when you think the dollar is going to go up. Theoretically you should want to be protected all the time, not just when you think the dollar is going up. The danger is that people will find religion on this subject when it happens to fit their view of the market.

But let's look at the flipside. Suppose we entered into a hedge of a hypothetical three-year foreign sourcing contract. We're short currencies, so we need to buy the currencies and sell dollars. As a result, we enter into a hedge on that firm commitment, as the accounting profession would refer to it. That is one that can be hedged under the FASB 52 rules.

Now we have sold dollars and the dollar falls a lot—let's say only a year into this three-year contract. Let's say it's moved from 160 to 120. Well, if it goes back up from there, the unrealized gains we have on those hedges will start to disappear.

But you might say, "120? Look at those gains. Well, I don't think I have this exposure anymore and I'm going to close out my hedge." Because you have been deferring the gain on the hedge, you now will take your gain into income in the quarter that you take off the hedge. If you happen to do that when earnings are under pressure for other reasons, well, isn't that nice?

That's the kind of thing that the accounting profession is worried about. All of a sudden, you could open the door to what is purely speculative activity and people could kind of come up with rationales why they need to do this or that. Or they may simply enter into bona fide hedges, and later have a change of heart about the problem. All of a sudden it may improve current earnings, so they take a hedge off. Admittedly, there is an earnings manipulation issue there.

So what do you think is the solution?

Fiedler: Well, we don't have a solution until accounting practice actually mirrors economic reality. Sooner or later, we have to figure out how we can get appropriate accounting treatment if we have hedged things that are real economic exposure. Manipulation of earnings or speculative abuses are a problem, but my belief is that is why you have accountants and auditors. That's part of their job—to be providing advice and counsel to corproations and not allowing inappropriate accounting treatment that can't be supported by the economic facts.

Does economic reality and hedging it make the accounting for hedging more difficult? Sure it does. But I don't see a way around that. That's life. Their concerns are legitimate, but the solution isn't to pretend the problem is not there.

Economic hedging, in terms of academic papers on the subject, has been out there a long time as an idea. Can you go back to meetings that you had that persuaded senior management to pursue the idea?

Fiedler: Operating management and senior management have been directly involved in those programs we have done to date. In that way, they get exposure to the ideas and they have seen what benefits these ideas offer over time.

But not all senior managers are sold on the idea, are they?

Hamilton: This is a comment I would make about U.S. companies in general. A lot of senior management probably have not had a lot of exposure to foreign exchange, other than knowing all those funny currencies somehow get translated into dollars. It's a bit of witchcraft to them.

Therefore, it's not surprsing that the senior management of many U.S. companies really do not have a lot of experience in that area. Most are not very well grounded in the principles and most have never dealt in it.

Fiedler: We talked earlier about accounting impact. Senior managers do tend to be very familiar with financial statements, but there's a distinction between that and the economic problem. They need to be educated and trained in economic issues that diverge, if you will, from accounting conventions.

Hamilton: Quarter to quarter translations in financial statements are pretty well understood. But the human factor plays a big part in all of this. You need some kind of experience before you will believe in any concept. That was our experience: it sounds like a good idea, but we are not sure that we totally understand the whole thing; but we basically trust you, so let's try it. What that gave us was an entrée to do some things, and then be able to report on them every six months or nine months. That just raised their whole consciousness about the issue.

When something works, I think it takes on a legitimacy that then is translated further into the organization. We have seen this—particularly as we have evolved where decisions we are making are moving further down in the organization. Now it's essential when some of these exchange hedging activities would impact a single business unit that we deal with the general manager of that business unit, not just with the CEO anymore.

So operating units now have a stake in decisions you make?

Fiedler: That's right. Whereas the tactical exposure is managed centrally, and accountability is here, that's not true with strategic exposures. We have defined those exposures as belonging to the operating units, not to treasury. As such, the decision makers are the operating managers, not the finance department.

Which also sounds like it's the politically correct thing to do too?

Hamilton: It is. And practically speaking too. If you think in terms of the various financial issues on a checklist that go into making a good decision, then you know it's not possible for financial decisions to be made separately and in a vacuum. They really are issues integrated with the operating units, and you need to approach them that way.

In reporting your results, what are the expectations?

Hamilton: It depends a bit on what the program is. But if it's a multi-year program, our experience has been that we will have a meeting once a year for sure, possibly two meetings, but not more than that. In our case, it would be a meeting with the finance committee, or the business unit general manager. To be more specific, the finance committee is made up of the CEO, president, and CFO. That would be the review committee that we have starting out.

Fiedler: In addition, I do have a responsiblity on a quarterly basis to report to Mike and other members of financial management to inform them about all aspects of the program. Mike would review the trading operation results, the results on tactical activity for the quarter, and all of the strategic programs that we have in place as well.

And how is the trading operation integrated with the strategic risk management program?

Fiedler: Actually, our three-man trading operation is off-line from the management of the corporation's exposures. But it's very integrally linked into our overall program, particularly in terms of market intelligence information flow and so forth.

Have things moved along to the point that your performance speaks for itself? What feedback do you get, or what attitudinal changes have you seen in those to whom you report?

Fiedler: In the early stages, it was understandable that we would run into some concern. But I don't think it's there anymore. As we are developing other programs, there's a comfort level building, a perception that the corporation has things under control. Among management, there's a feeling that this makes sense, that it's something we should be doing.

Hamilton: And that it really adds value. That's what has fundamentally changed over the last couple of years. There's a feeling here that this is a legitimate business-related activity, not some esoteric financial group off somewhere doing their own thing. Fundamentally, management knows that it will affect how well we compete.

Mike, how would you respond to the conservative chief executive officer at other companies who says, "We are in the widget business, not foreign exchange?"

Hamilton: I don't think you can operate in the world economy and not be in foreign exchange. I think that is putting your head in the sand. When you say you are in widgets, you've got some cost of widgets, and you've got some prices for widgets that you can charge. Likewise, your competition has widgets and they may have costs and prices in something other than dollars. If they do, then you are in the foreign exchange business, whether you want to be or not.

That's what fundamentally changed for Kodak. Top management at one time thought that managing foreign exchange was a nice thing for some group to do, but that it didn't really impact the business. They felt that we make film and, if finance wants to operate a profit-driven foreign exchange operation, fine. They probably know what they are doing, but we don't see how that can impact our core business. We haven't come to the end of the tunnel in trying to even further integrate the management of foreign exchange into the business operations of the company, but I think there's a much better understanding today than there used to be.

What do you see, Dave, in that regard?

Fiedler: You mentioned the term "more conservative." Very often what CEOs and other have in their minds when they think of foreign exchange is buy and sell—a trading kind of operation. They don't look at foreign exchange as an exposure management problem. In their minds, they are characterizing the problem in one way, "Yeah, banks do trading, but we don't need to." As if that's the problem.

What's missed are the economic linkages — the fundamental businesses and financial risks that any corporation faces. You hear a lot of financial people say, "We don't want to do options, that's risky." That's because they know you can lose money writing options, but in reality they can also lose money by not doing anything. That mentality is usually a function of not understanding what the foreign exchange markets are all about.

Hamilton: That's right. They relate foreign exchange to quote screens, telephones, noisy trading rooms, and buying and selling. That is the most visible part of these markets—how they operate. But what's missed is how these markets can be used to provide corporates with solutions.

Then I should get another perspective—should the shareholder should be more aware of these activities?

Hamilton: That's a tough question.

They have the myth of the foreign exchange markets, in the back of their minds, don't they?

Hamilton: Right. And analysts in general tend to focus on the accounting results, the quarterly earnings, the translation adjustment that comes about because of the accounting rules. I don't think they focus at all—at least the analysts that I know of—on the management of economic risk.

I agree with you that's something they should focus on, and it ought to be beneficial to the shareholder. How that gets communicated, I don't know. One of the things that worries me about even talking about this issue is that I look at this as giving us a competitive advantage. And I don't want to give that to anybody else. I agree with the statement that it clearly ought to be a beneficial activity from a shareholder's standpoint to understand this, but how you communicate that, I don't know. You won't find an analyst in a 1,000 that really understands this, and even fewer shareholders.

9

Baxter International

I thought there would be a lot of efficiency generated by having the same group monitor the financial marketplace and learn the theoretical techniques and financial tools to manage those risks. Given the magnitude of these exposures after the merger with American Hospital Supply, I knew we'd become proficient much more quickly if we had people managing these market risks on a full-time basis.

—BARBARA Y. MORRIS,
Treasurer
Baxter International

Figure 9.1   Baxter International Corporate Profile

Worldwide Sales of $8.1 billion	Products, Systems and Services			Major Customers
Hospital Products and Services 50.3%	MEDICAL PRODUCTS Procedure kits and trays Hypothermia and hyperthermia devices Nonwoven drapes and gowns Gloves Respiratory and anesthesia products Urological products Surgical instruments	IV SYSTEMS Intravenous (IV) solutions Premixed drugs in IV solutions Administration sets and catheters Flow control devices Nutritional products	CORPORATE SALES Corporate sales and agreements Multi-hospital systems sales DISTRIBUTION PRODUCTS Patient-care products Surgical supplies Textile products Dietary products Laboratory apparatus and supplies	HOSPITALS Pharmacy Operating room Materials management/central supply Administrative/CEO Laboratory BLOOD BANKS CLINICAL LABORATORIES ALTERNATE SITES Homes Dialysis centers Nursing homes Physicians' offices
Medical Systems and Specialties 21.3%	BLOOD THERAPY Collection and storage containers Component processing products Administration sets and filters Coagulation products Plasma volume expanders Immune globulin preparations	DIAGNOSTICS Clinical chemistry test systems Microbiology systems Immunochemistry systems Hematology systems Coagulation reagents	MEDICAL SPECIALTIES DEVICES Tissue and mechanical heart valves Cardiac monitoring systems Cardiac bypass systems	HOSPITALS Pharmacy Operating room Materials management/central supply Administrative/CEO Laboratory BLOOD BANKS ALTERNATE SITES Homes Dialysis centers Nursing homes Physicians' offices
Alternate Site Products and Services 22.5%	HOME CARE Kidney dialysis Nutrition therapy Antibiotic therapy Pain management therapy Chemotherapy	HEALTH COST MANAGEMENT Mail-order prescriptions Physical therapy services	ALTERNATE SITE DISTRIBUTION Medical supplies Veterinary supplies	ALTERNATE SITES Homes Dialysis centers Nursing homes Physicians' offices Corporations Dentists' offices
Industrial Products 5.9%	INDUSTRIAL Laboratory supplies, chemicals and equipment Industrial apparel Electrostatic-control supplies Clean-room apparel			INDUSTRIAL Research and educational laboratories Production facilities

Source: Baxter International Annual Reports

**Figure 9.2 Performance in Review:
Baxter International (1980–1989)**

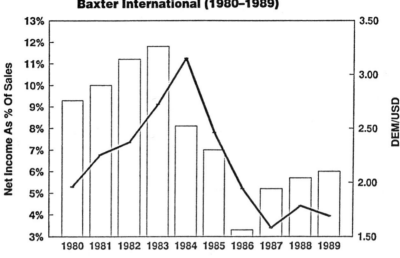

Baxter: A Bird's Eye View of Financial Risk

Unlike some corporations that tend to de-emphasize the role that treasury can play in improving the overall efficiency of global operations, Baxter International in Deerfield, Ill., views its treasury mission as a critical part of the company's overall success. Etched within a lucite triangle is the company's treasury mission statement. A key objective established by Robert J. Lambrix, chief financial officer at Baxter, reads: "To ensure the continued availability of financial resources required to fund the growth of Baxter's business in the most cost-effective manner." One of the ways in which Baxter meets this objective is by managing foreign exchange and interest rate exposures to take advantage of favorable market movements while protecting against market volatility.

Look at the evolution of the competitive environment faced by

Table 9.1   Performance in Review: Baxter International Income Statement (U.S. Dollars in Millions)

	1980	1981	1982	1983	1984
+ Sales	$1,374	$1,504	$1,671	$1,843	$1,800
− Cost of Goods Sold	($1,122)	($1,196)	($1,299)	(1,439)	($1,458)
Gross Profit	$253	$308	$373	$404	$342
Gross Profit %	18.4%	20.5%	22.3%	21.9%	19.0%
− Depreciation	($51)	($61)	($83)	($86)	($114)
− Other Costs	($43)	($58)	($58)	($48)	($58)
PBT	$159	$189	$232	$270	$170
− Taxes	($31)	($39)	($45)	($52)	($24)
Taxes %	-19.6%	-20.4%	-19.4%	-19.4%	-14.1%
Net Income	$128	$150	$187	$217	$146
Net Income %	9.3%	10.0%	11.2%	11.8	8.1%
Working Capital	$536	$607	$512	$461	$384
Working Capital/Sales %	39.0%	40.4%	30.6%	25.0%	21.3%
Long-term Debt	$273	$227	$167	$226	$206
Long-term Debt/Sales %	19.8%	15.1%	10.0%	12.2%	11.4%
Earnings Per Share	$0.93	$1.08	$1.32	$1.54	$1.03
Cash Flow Per Share	$1.29	$1.50	$1.91	$2.16	$1.83
Average Annual P/E	12.4	13.1	14.7	17.3	15.8

1985	1986	1987	1988	1989	Average	CAGR %
2,355	$5,543	$6,223	$6,861	$7,399	$3,657	20.6%
($1,964)	($4,833)	($5,283)	($5,846)	($6,200)	($3,064)	20.9%
$391	$710	$940	$1,015	$1,199	$593	18.9%
16.6%	12.8%	15.1%	14.8%	16.2%	17.8%	-1.4%
($134)	($285	($314	($335)	($436)	($190)	26.9%
($58)	($162)	($179)	($158)	($128)	($95)	13.0%
$199	$263	$447	$522	$634	$308	16.6%
($34)	($80)	($123)	($131)	($190)	($75)	22.3%
-17.0%	-30.4%	-27.6%	-25.1%	-30.0%	-22.3%	4.8%
$165	$183	$324	$391	$444	$234	14.8%
7.0%	3.3%	5.2%	5.7%	6.0%	7.8%	-4.8%
$1,145	$463	$881	$1,437	$1,565	$799	12.7%
48.6%	8.4%	14.2%	20.9%	21.2%	27.0%	-6.6%
$2,580	$1,568	$1,658	$2,246	$2,052	$1,120	25.1%
109.6%	28.3%	26.6%	32.7%	27.7%	29.4%	3.8
$1.04	$0.64	$1.10	$1.31	$1.50	$1.15	5.5%
$1.39	$1.88	$2.40	$2.69	$3.29	$2.03	11.0%
14.0	28.5	22.1	15.8	14.4	16.8	1.7%

Baxter in the last decade, and this objective begins to make sense. Since 1983, dramatic changes have taken place in the healthcare industry—particularly in how patients are treated and how providers would be reimbursed for the associated cost of such services. Significant cost containment efforts by national governments and other healthcare payors are forcing the restructuring of healthcare delivery systems, adding pressure on hospitals, and increasing the number of out-patient and alternate-site treatments. The focus—cost effectivness and quality.

In particular, these changes in the U.S. market began when the U.S. Congress decided to limit reimbursement for treatment of Medicare patients. The previous system reimbursed hospitals for the reasonable cost of services. Under the prospective reimbursement system, hospitals are reimbursed at a fixed rate based on the patient's particular diagnosis, regardless of the actual costs incurred.

Others have followed the lead of Congress. Most private healthcare payors have adopted similar reimbursement plans and are providing other incentives for consumers to seek lower cost care outside the hospital. Corporate health plans have been restructured to provide financial incentives for patients to utilize the most cost-effective forms of treatments. Managed care programs, such as health maintenance organizations (HMOs), have become more popular, and physicians have been encouraged to provide more cost-effective treatment.

Baxter has responded positively in the last decade to these pressures with a number of operational moves to enhance its competitiveness through diversification. Baxter is engaged in the worldwide development, manufacture, and distribution of a diversified line of products, systems and services used primarily in the health-care field. Products are manufactured by the company in 23 countries and sold in approximately 100 countries. The company's more than 120,000 products are used principally by hospitals, clinical and medical research laboratories, blood and dialysis centers, rehabilitation centers, nursing homes, doctors' offices, and at home under physician supervision.

The company now maintains 53 manufacturing facitilities in the U.S., including 11 in Puerto Rico, and also manufacturers in Australia, Belgium, Brazil, Canada, Colombia, Costa Rica, the Dominican Republic, France, Germany, Ireland, Italy, Japan, Malaysia, Malta, Mexico, the Netherlands, Scotland, Singapore, Spain, Switzerland, and the United Kingdom.

This global network was enhanced on November 25, 1985, when Baxter acquired American Hospital Supply Corp. in a purchase transaction valued at approximately $3.7 billion. The acquisition allowed Baxter to transform itself from a relatively focused company generating $1.4 billion in sales through its sterile fluid, blood collection, kidney dialysis and bloodfraction businesses into a company which today generates $8.1 billion in sales from a broad line of hospital products used in dialysis centers, blood banks and diagnostic labs.

Such a bold move was not without its own financial risks. To complete this acquistion, Baxter took on an additional $2.0 billion in debt. Currently, $1.3 billion of $2.2 billion overall is floating rate debt. As interest rates rise, so does the company's interest expense—unless, of course, it has taken action to manage this exposure.

And that it does. Baxter utilizes financial futures, options, and interest rate caps to minimize the company's exposure to adverse movments in interest rates related to commercial paper, short-term notes, and anticipated long-term debt issuances. In 1988, for example, Baxter had hedged $800 million of a $1.1 billion exposure to floating interest rates by virtue of its commercial paper portfolio. By 1989, interest rates rose from a level of roughly 7.5 percent—the level at which the caps were done—to the point that all of Baxter's interest rate cap positions were significantly in-the-money.

In addition, Baxter has strategically incorporated imbedded option-features into its bonds to lower its cost of funds. In 1988, for example, the company issued bonds that offered put and call features to investors. One particular issue of $100 million offered investors a five-year put and Baxter a 10-year call. In exchange for selling the investor an option to redeem the bond in five years if interest rates rise, Baxter lowered its cost of funds by an estimated 20 basis points.

In addition to managing its interest rate exposure, a treasury team that includes Lambrix; Barbara Y. Morris, treasurer since 1986; Barbara Byrnes, Assistant Treasurer; and Robert J. Danko, corporate finance manager, also jointly manage the company's foreign exchange exposure. The opportunity to see both exposures in tandem within a highly centralized treasury operation is a bird's eye view afforded to few treasury operations in corporate America.

On the foreign exchange side, Baxter's treasury group manages exposures resulting from approximately $2 billion in international sales. These transactional and firm commitment exposures can be hedged up to one year out through the use of forward contracts and currency options. During 1988 and 1989, Baxter made extensive use of these option-based strategies to hedge itself against currency volatility.

Minimizing this volatility is critical since Baxter operates in such a competitive pricing environment within the hospital supply industry. Baxter is in the strong position of being able to help hospitals achieve savings by optimizing the economies of scale associated with aggregating supply purchases, by recognizing increasing efficiencies within its manufacturing operations, and by reducing its own exposures to foreign exchange risk and interest expenses when necessary.

Merrill Lynch analysts Lucy E. Olwel and Jean L. Queally in their research about the company's prospects said: "Baxter's future growth should come from operating profit gains in excess of 15 percent, rather than the non-operating gains that had supported Baxter's bottomline growth during the past several years. . . we believe that the quality of Baxter's earnings will improve since future EPS growth is based on operating income growth and not non-recurring gains."

As Baxter's treasury team points out in this interview, the company must continue to pay close attention to the negative impact a strong dollar or high interest rates can have on its products in global markets. In addition, they discuss the hedging and funding strategies that allow them to combat such potential risks.

Interview: Barbara Y. Morris, Barbara Byrnes, Robert J. Danko

What was the impetus for starting sophisticated hedging programs at Baxter?

Byrnes: I joined in 1980, when the foreign exchange group was up and running and doing fairly similar activities to what we are doing today. I'm sure that most of their activities focused on the floating of the dollar back in 1973. When I joined in 1980, we were very focused on this risk, and still are.

On the interest rate side, we started actively managing our exposure in 1985 when the company merged with American Hospital Corp. The merger increased our debt to $2.5 billion. That was enough to catch anybody's attention. When you are looking at a merger with that much debt, the risks are quite substantial. That certainly raised the visibility of managing interest rate risk dramatically, although we had looked at the issue in prior years.

Danko: Further, in addition, there were covenants in the borrowing facility that a specified amount of debt must have its interest rate fixed for a certain amount of time. The banks obviously were mindful of a rate rise.

Byrnes: I believe forty percent of the floating rate debt had to be protected—that is, hedged or fixed. At that time, the only alternative was the swap market. Soon after the merger, however, other markets became available. But swaps were all we had at the time besides doing a fixed rate bond issue.

How big is your debt portfolio?

Byrnes: It's ranged anywhere from $2.2 billion to $2.7 billion over the last several years. At least a billion of that at any given time has been short-term domestic floating rate debt. Sometimes more.

So your greatest fear is rising interst rates?

Byrnes: Well, yes, but in looking at the portfolio overall, if rates go down, you have a risk as well on the fixed portfolio—an opportunity cost. That is something we have watched closely.

Morris: Sometimes we have called bonds.

Is it typical that companies start out doing these activities when they are being hurt? For example, when you go back to the 1970s, was the company losing money in foreign exchange? Or was treasury proactive enough to manage the problem before it even emerged?

Morris: I think that some companies have been proactive. I would expect in the mid-1970s, when the dollar was allowed to float, that many treasuries did sensitivity analyses to currency fluctuations. Once the dollar was allowed to float for a while, I think they began to see how volatile it was going to be. They could see this was a very different world in which they were now going to operate.

It was no different at Baxter. If you were a company like Baxter at the time, your exposure to the dollar was increasing. By the time we got to the merger, our international sales were close to 30 percent of our total. That exposure had been gradually increasing over time and we could clearly see its implications. So, I don't think you have to get hurt to recognize this is a real issue. Leadership companies anticipate these types of impacts and develop strategies to manage them. On the interest rate side, many companies have also been proactive. They recognized the potential volatility. I think there are companies that do it because they could not withstand the potential volatility.

A lot of what Baxter did was just to learn about the mechanics and to get some experience, so if there was a time when hedging this exposure would be critical, we would be prepared.

Byrnes: Yes, I can remember a study that someone in treasury had done back in 1980 or 1981—a man by the name of Chuck Thurman.

It was an extensive study and analysis of how to hedge using the futures markets. It discussed hedging a commerical paper portfolio using Eurodollar futures, which started trading at the Chicago Mercantile Exchange around that time.

Tell me about Mr. Thurman. Who is he?

Morris: He's now our vice president of financial relations and handles the investor relations activities. It's not uncommon for people with the treasury background to circulate through that area of responsiblity because of their capabilities in dealing with external constituencies such as bankers. His responsibility now happens to be with investment analysts, and has been since 1983.

Tell me a little more about this pilot research that treasury initially did?

Byrnes: It was really done to try to get a better handle on how the actual futures markets worked, and what type of things we would have to do day-to-day to see if futures were effective in offsetting commercial paper risk.
Morris: It also identified how you actually implement such transactions. It dealt with issues such as how you determine the relationship between Treasury bill futures and the underlying cash instrument in our care—the basis risk issue.

For how long did you research this subject? Was treasury actually initiating a pilot hedging program, or was it just research?

Byrnes: Research.
Morris: He was simply educating all of us. It sounded pretty magical at that point. A lot of his energy was spent educating people like me on how interest rate hedging was supposed to work. We needed to expose the treasurer and other senior finance managers to

157

the issues related to interest rate hedging. Ultimately, that paid off in persuading senior management to buy into the idea and to initiate a hedging program with some degree of comfort.

So when was the buyout? And did it push the concept of managing interest rate risk along a little quicker?

Morris: With the anticipated merger with American Hospital Supply merger on November 25, 1985. I still remember the day.

And Mr. Thurman's research got you started hedging?

Byrnes: It certainly provided a framework. However, I think it was also our overall experience in hedging foreign exchange exposures that allowed us to go into the interest rate area with ease. That experience made the concept of hedging interest rates easier for senior management to understand.

Can you explain why the world is a riskier place from your company's perspective?

Morris: Our marketplace is putting greater and greater constraints upon us. Since 1983 when the government instituted diagnostic related groups (DRGs), the hospital supply business has changed. The government now reimburses on the basis of target rates which it establishes when you are on Medicare, instead of reimbursing on a cost plus basis to the hospital.

For example, before 1983, hospitals had established that it actually cost $1,000 for a certain medical procedure and we reimbursed on that basis. Now the government's DRG is saying it *should* cost $850 and reimbursement is at that level. The hospitals have responded in several ways.

From our perspective, the most significant thing they have done is try to rachet back on their expenses such as product costs. We have never had exorbitant price increases but the reduced flexibility to do so just put that much more pressure on our side of the equation. As a result, we had much less ability to absorb potential interest rate volatility.

Many risk managers say Baxter is unique because it manages both foreign exchange and interest rate exposures together. Why did you organize your treasury operation in that way?

Morris: When I accepted this position, it just intuitively made sense to me. If you look at what drives foreign exchange and interest rates, it's the same factors, whether it's the economic conditions, the political environment, or central bank activity in various countries. Key indicators which you would watch for foreign exchange would also be critical for interest rates.

I noticed that because I used to walk around in the morning visiting people who cover interest rates and people who watch foreign exchange. It was always interesting to see if they highlighted the same capital market/political activities—generally they did.

Also, the hedging tools that you use to manage these risks are very similar. They may be called something different, but whether it's futures or forwards or swaps you are doing the same thing. And if it's options, the range forward contract is really just a combination of two options, buying a put option and selling a call option.

I thought there would be a lot of efficiency generated by having the same group monitor the financial marketplace and learn the theoretical techniques and financial tools to manage those risks. Given the magnitude of these exposures after the merger with American Hospital Supply, I knew we'd become proficient much more quickly if we had people managing these market risks on a full-time basis.

Byrnes: The markets are global now and that influenced how we are structured. Barbara looked at it and saw the potential inefficiency of having two groups. For example, if you borrow U.S. dollars for the parent company in Europe, should the transaction be done by the international treasury group or the domestic treasury group?

At a point six or seven years ago, companies typically decided whether they were going to do the financing in the U.S. or overseas. Today, however, you want to be in a position where when you are ready to finance, look at the global capital markets, say, "OK, where's the best rate?", and then pull the trigger. This structure reflects a desire to have a global decision-making process in terms of financing.

To be frank about it, you also had the domestic and international groups both doing analyses related to borrowing in their respective marketplace. When you selected the marketplace in which to do the transaction, the other team feels disheartened because it was as though their efforts were for naught. So why not have one group overlook all of these markets at once?

When has this merger of domestic and international exposure management functions paid off?

Morris: For example, we went through an evaluation of Euro-commercial paper, as have a lot of other companies. Barbara and her group didn't have any vested interest in the outcome of the evaluation of whether we should move from the domestic to the Euro-commercial paper market. I'm convinced that if that evaluation had been done by a separate international treasury group, it would have been more difficult to maintain that objectivity. The domestic group would have wanted U.S. commercial paper, and the international group would have wanted Euro-commercial paper. After all, it's a natural reaction.

Barbara, how much of their time is devoted to financing and risk management actitivities?

Morris: They tell me 130 percent, but I think it's probably more like 60 percent.

So what do they do with the rest of their time?

Morris: Seriously, they spend all their time doing those activities. And that adds value.

Instead of having assistant treasurers, domestic and international, devoting portions of their time to these capital market activities, this structure provided more focus at a time when financial exposure to management was critical to the company's success.

Danko: There are other advantages as well. The question about borrowing short-term versus long-term isn't a politically charged issue. Everything is driven by the source and the ultimate use of the funds, not by who is making a transaction.

Byrnes: There are companies that do distinguish between long and short-term. Anything less than "X" months is put in one area, and anything longer in another.

Morris: People are very surprised that we put commercial paper in with everything else. They are very surprised it isn't in the domestic treasury area. Again, the reason is that I want the same people involved in commercial paper issuance to do the interest rate hedging, when that strategy is appropriate.

Byrnes: That's the distinction we can make from our vantage point. Parent company financing such as commercial paper and public offerings are the responsibility of the capital markets area, and international subsidiary financing is in the international treasury domain.

What has your treasury operation done that has really helped the company's overall performance and efficiency? Are there any war stories that you can tell?

Byrnes: I look at 1988 as our important time. It was an exceptional year for us.

We did interest rate hedges using caps as well as straight Eurodollar options, which proved to be very valuable to us. At that time, there had not been a lot of corporations active in that market. Many companies simply weren't willing to use straight Eurodollar options to hedge their exposures. The interest rate cap market wasn't as liquid as it was today.

We hedged a portion of our commercial paper and the timing was good. We not only hedged our 1988 exposures but also, in the middle of the year, hedged a portion of our 1989 exposure.

Those transactions had an interesting twist. Here it was May or June of 1988, and we were hedging our 1989 exposure but didn't want to increase the amount hedged for the remainder of 1988. The solution was caps with a delayed start. They weren't actually effective for six months. With the cap market we were relatively thin at the time—it was definitely not a commercial paper-type market—it was a substantial challenge to achieve our objective.

On the foreign exchange side, we also used some currency options in 1987 to hedge our exposures that were quite successful.

What was the secret to making such good decisions?

Morris: Our biggest advantage was synergy. I don't know if we would have gotten nearly as far along with interest rate hedging if we hadn't lumped it together with foreign exchange. After the merger, we moved quickly with interest rate hedging. We talked about more sophisticated option strategies—different ways to mix buying and selling put and call options to generate participating and range forward option strategies. We implemented a number of these combination strategies.

In terms of educating ourselves and senior management with all of these techniques on the foreign exchange side, we made a lot of progress. Bob would walk into my office and say we should do an interest rate collar. It is just like a foreign exchange range foward. The lingo may be a little different, but the mechanics of the transaction are not. Because we had been very aggressive in considering new techniques to apply to foreign exchange, I knew that we could move very quickly if the same mechanism was appropriate for interest rates. In some cases, as with interest rate collars, a lot of their value comes from the shape of the yield curve. If you don't move quickly, you may lose your chance. The most significant synergy I saw was educating ourselves on the foreign exchange side so that we could respond much more quickly to opportunities on the interest rate side. And I'm sure there will be opportunities in the opposite direction in the future as market conditions change.

How quickly can you make a decision to hedge? What sort of time-frames are we talking about in terms of speed, and how might this contrast with the speed of other corporations in making similar decisions?

Byrnes: It depends on where you are in the year, your hedging time horizon, and what you are looking to do. If it is a five-year transaction involving some type of creative swap, that will probably take a little longer than if it was hedging an exposure out to the end of the year.

So speed isn't always of the essence.

Morris: It can be. For example, the interest collar did evolve very quickly. These two came to me in the morning insisting on lunch with Bob Lambrix.

Byrnes: Yes, we had spent the previous six to 12 months educating people about the transaction and several months monitoring market conditions.

Morris: The education process, by the way, was one of the biggest secrets and was the reason for its success.

Byrnes: Yes, because of the yield curve conditions, we knew at the time opportunities would be coming down the road to do a costless option transaction with no upfront premium to hedge our exposures.

We kept seeing the yield curve invert, and invert, and invert even more, and we had explained what that meant to senior management.

Finally, one day we received a call here about pricing a two-year range which we had been monitoring. That morning, Bob and I interrupted a meeting in Barbara's office. We passed her a piece of paper which said: Here is a 9 percent and 7 5/8 percent free range for 1990 and 1991. Barbara's eyes lit up. We ended up having lunch with the CFO. We discussed the parameters with him and he said yes.

What you are telling me is that you had been watching the potential possibility of this transaction for a long time?

Byrnes: Not this transaction specifically—but we had been watching the collar market because we had seen opportunities there. We were just trying to find the right time to get the best range that we could.

Tell me about the education process and why it is important to doing successful transactions.

Morris: We have a financing committee and a foreign exchange committee. We meet quarterly with each group, and Barbara and Bob use these meetings to educate the rest of us.

Typically, these meetings will include the senior tax officer, the controller and the chief financial officer, as well as legal counsel. As soon as Barbara and Bob find something interesting in the marketplace, they talk to us about it. And sometimes they talk to us several times. So when we recommend a transaction, people feel very comfortable with it. That's always an advantage when you are trying to sell an idea.

Obviously, not every decision you make will be a correct one. So how do you deal with reporting to management and monitoring postions?

Byrnes: You have to remember that we have an underlying exposure on the opposite side of these hedge transactions. So, you have to look at all of the pieces. And you may have a lot of hedges in place at once. When we make the decision to hedge an exposure, it's because we are happy to lock in at that specific rate.

How do you establish the financing rate with which you're comfortable?

Byrnes: It's always 50 basis points under market (Laughs). Seriously, that depends on where rates are at any given point in time, and if we actually want to fix or do a bond issue. We have flexibility with regard to time when we finance or refinance a maturing bond. Therefore, we have the flexibility to watch the markets, to get an idea of where rates may be moving and what shape the yield curve may be taking.

Danko: We do spend quite a lot of time quantifying what the exposures are, both the interest rate and foreign exchange. We always look at the impact of different rate scenarios. We always have a sense of our overall sensitivity to financial risk. We use that information to manage our exposures at a level where we are comfortable.

When we decide to hedge or fix rates, our philosophy is to average into the market. You never really know if you got a good rate until the bond matures and you can reflect back on just how opportune your timing was.

So we try to average in. Even though we felt we got some fantastic rates in Fall 1989, our philosophy was to sit tight for six months and then decide if we wanted to do additional hedges. We don't want to put all our eggs in one basket.

Let's switch to foreign exchange exposures for a moment. Have you started managing long-dated economic exposures, as some have done?

Byrnes: Since the SEC pronouncement, I don't believe anyone is actually hedging these exposures for, say, five years and deferring hedge contract gains and losses.

Really?

Byrnes: If companies hedge long-term economic exposures they take on the volatility in reported earnings of marking multi-year contracts to market. They are economically hedged, but it's the hedge accounting treatment that is crucial to many corporations. If, for example, you are hedging for a five-year horizon, corporations want the first year of the hedge offset against year one, the second year for year two, and so on. That way, within each one-year time period, you are matching your exposure with your hedge.

So how far was Baxter going out? Or do you do it yearly based on a budget?

Byrnes: We have not gotten into the long-dated transactions for foreign exchange.

Morris: But theoretically we do go out 2 or 3 years on the interest rate side.

Byrnes: On the interest rate side—yes, definitely. But not with foreign exchange risk.

Why's that?

Morris: Current accounting practices have discouraged us from doing anything further than that for foreign exchange.

If you could do an economic hedging program, without facing all of the accounting confusion that potentially exists, would you do it?

Morris: Prior to the SEC announcement, we had brought in some outside experts who spent some time with us and our international operating management on just this type of program. One of Bob's 1989 objectives was analyzing of our overseas subsidiaries, with regard to specific product line, to try to anticipate what the flows would be over a three- to five-year period. We wanted to see if we could identify what the potential currency risks were. We never finished that project because of the pronouncement. But before that, the idea had generated a lot of internal interest.

What products does the company have that you are interested in hedging from a strategic point of view, in terms of protecting margins? Was it a specific product that you were thinking about?

Morris: Yes, it was. I won't tell you which one for competitive reasons, but it was one in which we had pretty high margins and felt that we had a competitive advantage. It's only in products where you have a franchise to protect and a favorable position with the dollar relative to some other currency that you would be willing to consider a three- or five-year hedge.

What's the next best alternative, given the current accounting situation?

Morris: There's nothing you can do long-term and be assured of favorable accounting treatment given the current accounting situation. But you can hedge foreign exchange risk on an annual basis.

Are your hedging programs based on an ability to forecast? Or do you take a perspective that your forecasting abilities are limited?

Morris: Different people here come out in different places on that question. Barbara and I are probably at opposite ends of the spectrum. Bob is probably in the middle.

Danko: I really take no view.

Byrnes: Again, there's a budget level that we use at the beginning of the year, and we try to make sure that the company does not get adversely affected by the dollar strengthening beyond that point.

Morris: In my own mind, I try not to be held captive to the budget, although it's easy to do. Your responses should be based more on what you really think is going to happen. I'm of the opinion that I'm not smart enough about anticipating the market, but Barbara and Bob Lambri can figure it out.

Danko: I'm in the middle. Over the long term you can't consistently outperform the market.

Let's pick on Barbara for a moment. What makes you so confident you can call the market?

Byrnes: The other Barbara says that, I didn't.

Morris: Yes, she tells me she can.

Byrnes: There's a point I'd like to make. We are not calling the markets here. But having been in the market for a long time, maybe I'm not so good on the six to 12-month trends, but my averages have been pretty good over a shorter period of time. We invariably get nervous when the dollar strengthens four pfennings in a very short period of time.

Morris: We meaning me. I know what all this "we" business means.

Byrnes: They do call it executive level syndrome. They start calling you, because all of a sudden they start watching and saying sell now, when soon it will be a time to buy. The feeling is that, if it's taken the currencies that amount of time to get to this point, it will turn around and go the other way.

So, will you be a little more conservative in your tendency to overreact?

Byrnes: That's right. But you must also realize that it may not always be helpful to have my background in foreign exchange and banking. Opinionated views sometimes have drawbacks when you are making decisions to manage risk.

If you were to consider your debt exposure in relation to foreign exchange exposures, which is a larger priority?

Morris: That's hard to say. We have a lot more debt than we do foreign exchange exposure. But the foreign exchange can be much more volatile.

Byrnes: That's true. You can see a 1 percent move in currencies in two days, whereas you won't see such volatility in interest rates.

So how do you collect exposure information?

Morris: Much of it is done by faxes. It's really tough, though, because you're dealing with subsidiaries around the world and the last thing they want from headquarters is a fax saying that they need to send more information on potential foreign exchange exposures.

Do they do any hedging?

Byrnes: No.

Morris: The problem—and we debate this topic internally about twice a year, as do most companies—is that if they hedge themselves, they would ultimately end up hedging against one other. Because we have a lot of intercompany payments, we are able to net all the exposures against one another, and hedge the net company exposure. There's a strong economic argument for keeping treasury activities centrally orchestrated.

In terms of a currency hedge that you've done, does one stand out?

Morris: In 1988, on December 4th or the 5th, which day was it?

Byrnes: The 5th.

Morris: Yes. On December 4, 1988, we decided we were going to hedge our 1989 foreign exchange exposure, and the timing couldn't have been better. It was the low point of the dollar for that period.

169

Byrnes: I think we were off by 24 hours of hitting the absolute low for the dollar up to that point. That was phenomenal.

Morris: That was just a stroke of pure luck, although Barbara tells me it's genius. We hedged all of our exposures for 1989. The problem is, frankly, that it worked out almost too well. There was such an economic advantage to doing this hedge that the senior management said, "OK, that's great for 1989, but what are you going to do for 1990?" By managing an exposure extremely well, you create a bogey that is difficult to match each year. It's can be a catch-22.

Why exactly was it such a good year?

Byrnes: We used the range option concept because of the historic interest rate differentials between the dollar and the yen, and the dollar and the mark. Those differentials really made range forwards an excellent choice, as the inverted yield curve had on the interest rate side.

Are you hedging only foreign sales, or what would be fair game?

Morris: Anything potentially.
Byrnes: But mostly exports.

What are your largest currency exposures?

Morris: The European currencies are far and away the largest. We also have exposure to the yen, the Canadian dollar, and pound sterling.

Barbara, what would cause you or Bob Lambrix to reject an idea that the other Barbara or Bob may propose?

Morris: I'll give you an example. Bob and I have talked about this because he came up with a very creative scheme to hedge our Canadian dollar exposure. Instead of using forwards, for which you incurred an immediate disadvantage because interest rates in Canada were higher than ours, Bob had a fairly intricate strategy using a combination of options.

There was an economic benefit to doing that under various scenarios. I didn't think there was enough economic value added to make the more complex strategy worth it. For that amount of effort, I thought that we could add more economic value someplace else. I really liked the idea and applauded his creativity. If it was the yen, for example, and the potential dollar pick up would have been more significant, we probably would have done it. We think in those terms about most every transaction—the best case, the worst case, and the most likely payoff.

Are hedging positions aggregated and managed on a portfolio basis?

Byrnes: We don't look at individual invoices, if that's what you mean. We aggregate data from the operating units and consolidate from a global perspective.

In terms of currency hedging, since you had such a good year in 1988, what sort of rationale have you tried to impose on the committees that evaluate your strategies and performance?

Byrnes: We told them that was a one-time event. Since we established our budget rate, one or two of the currencies have moved very much in our favor on the larger exposures, so we added value again in 1989 relative to the budget rates.

10

Pitney Bowes, Inc.

We believe, because we have an outstanding service and sales organization, that we bring that to the marketplace better than anybody else. That's our operating advantage. That's our added value. Therefore, whenever we can lock up some favorable currency to what we believe our budget is, and of course our budget rate is an acceptable operating level target, we think it gives us an additional competitive advantage and that we can go in there and get closer to our competitors on price.

—Carmine F. Adimando
> *Vice President—Finance and Administration and Treasurer,*
> Pitney Bowes, Inc.

We are not a profit center. We are here just to minimize risk. We are not trying to second guess the operating units. But if they come in on a Friday afternoon and the markets are thin, I may not want to trade at that point. I'll wait for a more opportune time. Since I'm giving an average for the entire year, there are some months that I would be forced to cover at a loss if I simply took the rate I gave them. So I try not to cover anything at a loss—even if it's just a very small gain, or break even, that's OK. I just trying to maximize the opportunities for the company.

—Mary Jo Abate
> *Assistant Treasurer,* Pitney Bowes, Inc.

Table 10.1 Performance in Review: Pitney Bowes Income Statement (U.S. Dollars in Millions)

	1980	1981	1982	1983	1984
+ Sales	$1,257	$1,414	$1,455	$1,607	$1,732
− Cost of Goods Sold	($1,062)	($1,219)	($1,257)	(1,348)	($1,450)
Gross Profit	$195	$195	$198	$259	$282
Gross Profit %	15.5%	13.8%	13.6%	16.1%	16.3%
− Depreciation	($60)	($67)	($72)	($76)	($86)
− Other Income & Costs	$4	$9	$25	$48	$60
PBT	$139	$137	$151	$231	$256
− Taxes	($63)	($68)	($68)	($114)	($117)
Taxes %	-45.7%	-49.5%	-45.1%	-49.2%	-45.8%
Net Income	$75	$69	$83	$117	$139
Net Income %	6.0%	4.9%	5.7%	7.3%	8.0%
Working Capital	$176	$191	$208	$176	$181
Working Capital/Sales %	14.0%	13.5%	14.3%	10.9%	10.4%
Long-term Debt	$146	$160	$159	$145	$147
Long-term Debt/Sales %	11.6%	11.3%	10.9%	9.0%	8.5%
Earnings Per Share	$1.08	$0.95	$1.08	$1.51	$1.75
Cash Flow Per Share	$2.17	$2.01	$2.29	$2.74	$3.07
Average Annual P/E	8.1	7.5	7.6	9.9	9.1

1985	1986	1987	1988	1989	Average	CAGR %
1,832	$1,987	$2,251	$2,650	$2,876	$1,906	9.6%
($1,557)	($1,647)	($1,859)	($1,958)	($2,082)	($1,544)	7.8%
$275	$340	$392	$692	$794	$362	16.9%
15.0%	17.1%	17.4%	26.1%	27.6%	17.9%	6.6%
($104)	($123)	($143)	($166)	($195)	($109)	14.0%
$86	$94	$96	($163)	($227)	$3	
$257	$311	$345	$362	$372	$256	11.6%
($112)	($144)	($144)	($126)	($119)	($108)	7.2%
-43.7%	-46.3%	-41.9%	-34.9%	-31.9%	-43.1%	-3.9%
$145	$167	$200	$236	$253	$148	14.4%
7.9%	8.4%	8.9%	8.9%	8.8%	7.5%	4.3%
$137	$120	$172	$334	$572	$227	14.0%
7.5%	6.0%	7.6%	12.6%	19.9%	11.7%	4.0%
$155	$174	$288	$1,102	$1,447	$392	29.0%
8.4%	8.8%	12.8%	41.6%	50.3%	17.3%	17.7%
$1.83	$2.10	$2.53	$3.00	$3.18	$1.90	12.7%
$3.26	$3.73	$4.47	$5.15	$5.70	$3.46	11.3%
11.3	14.4	16.2	14.3	14.7	11.3	6.8%

Figure 10.1 Performance in Review:
Pitney Bowes (1981-1989)

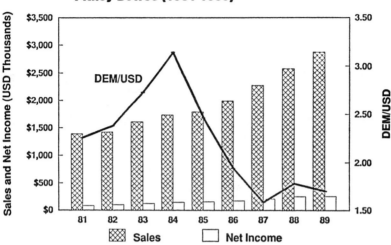

Source: Pitney Bowes Annual Reports

Pitney Bowes: Strategically Managing Its Cost of Capital

Pitney Bowes is a leading supplier of mailing equipment, facsimile machines, copiers, dictation equipment, and retail price marketing and bar code equipment with $2.9 billion in annual sales. In recent years, the company has been applying the excess cash flow from its core postage meter business to expand in high-growth related areas where its existing strengths can be utilized. Its large market shares in mailing equipment and voice processing systems provide an entry for its copier and facsimile machines products among business customers. An extensive equipment servicing organization and its large finance operation are important competitive advantages.

Figure 10.2 Pitney Bowes: European Profitability Versus USD/DM Changes

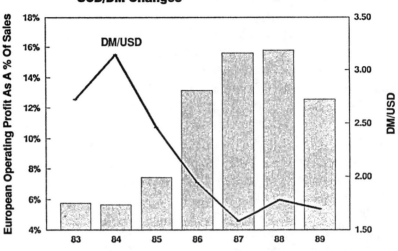

Its business equipment division generated 74 percent of revenues and 51 percent of operating profits in 1989; business supplies and services division, 10 percent of revenues and 12 percent of operating profits; and financial services, 16 percent of revenues and 37 percent of operating profits. As a result of aggressive expansion overseas, appoximately 25 percent of the companies revenues are generated outside the U.S. Pitney Bowes' performance continues to be strong. In 1989, for the eighth consecutive year, the company increased its common stock dividend. Likewise, it retains its AA–rating from both Moody's and Standard and Poor's, due to its sound financial condition and performance.

Key to its ability to compete globally, however, has been its strategic reorganization to automate the mailing and shipping businesses—and to move into complimentary "mailroom" businesses. Since 1986, the company has spent well over $250 million to apply software and computer technology to mailing and shipping equipment. In addition, its copier division has targeted metropolitan areas as a focal point and continues to emphasize Pitney Bowes' specialty—higher margin support services and supplies for commercial accounts.

Overseeing the financial side of Pitney Bowes' strategic plan to automate mailrooms and offices around the world is Carmine F. Adimando, vice president-finance and administration and treasurer. Adimando serves as the company's chief financial officer and is responsible for all treasury and pension-related activities, as well as investor relations. On financing and financial risk management activities for the company, Adimando works with Assistant Treasurer Mary Jo Abate, who helps manage international treasury operations.

Adimando joined Pitney Bowes in 1979 after holding positions with American Airlines, Inc., Burndy Corporation, and Deloitte, Haskins & Sells. He became vice president of finance in June 1987. Along with Abate, former director of corporate treasury at Schering Plough Corp. in Madison, New Jersey, Adimando has instituted new methods to manage interest rate and currency exposures at Pitney Bowes.

Pitney Bowes' strategy is to have treasury set budgeted rates for the year for each country—rates the operating units must utilize. The operating general managers then have the opportunity to request a hedge on their requirements for either part or all of the year. In the U.K., for example, Pitney Bowes may give a British subsidiary an exchange rate of 1.63 to buy from other operating units for the entire year. As a "bank to the subs", Adimando and Abate are then left to manage the exposure created for centralized treasury operations in Stanford, Conn. The objective is to make exposure to foreign currencies work in Pitney Bowes' favor and to relieve local management of treasury concerns.

After giving an average rate to its subsidaries, Pitney Bowes then tries to maximize the potential opportunities associated with the exposure. The objective is always to avoid currency losses. Pitney Bowes executes approximately $400 million in forward and spot transactions to hedge foreign exchange exposures per year. Part of Pitney Bowes's success has come from the ability to consolidate banking relationships more direct market intelligence which has resulted in. While Pitney Bowes once worked with as many as 25 banks, foreign exchange risk is now manage through five to eight banks.

In addition to centralized exposure management and hedging, Pitney Bowes endeavors to centralize cash management wherever possible, particularly within countries where there are multiple subsidiaries. In the U.K., for example, Pitney Bowes subsidiaries pool their funds before any of them invest or borrow externally. Once netting has taken place, all hedges are related to transactional exposures that remain. For settlement of the internal exposures, Pitney Bowes makes use of an internal netting system to avoid currency deal-making with banks. Through a netting system with a bank in Amsterdam, the company's operating units offset their intercompany payables, settling the net exposure in their own currency. The contracts with corporate treasury are included in this settlement. If the subsidiaries have forecasted poorly or increased their currency requirements, the bank buys or sells the difference.

Pitney Bowes' currency exposures are somewhat unique. With over 20 percent of it revenues coming from overseas sales, it has net long exposures in Canadian dollars, pound sterling, and Deutsche marks. Equipment purchasing from Japan, on the other hand, leaves it with a net short position in Japanese yen.

Pitney Bowes also has interest rate exposures that must be managed. The company's commercial paper program has grown as high as $330 million for corporate and $750 million for its Financial Services operations. As a result, Pitney Bowes has made use of no-cost collar transactions and callable swaps as hedges. In March 1989, for example, Pitney Bowes entered into a five-year interest rate swap agreement that converted the five-year, floating-rate debt into a fixed-rate debt. The swap's callable feature was a new wrinkle that allowed the bank to reverse the swap back in three years, if rates were favorable. In return, Pitney Bowes received a sizable premium that reduced its financing costs well below market rates.

At the end of June 1989, Pitney Bowes entered into a $10 million, no-cost collar to put a ceiling on commercial paper rates. Abate refused to comment on what rate she specifically placed the ceiling, but the ceiling—an option—is finance by selling a floor—another option—to the bank. At that time, for example, a bank may have offered a no-cost collar of 7 percent and 9 percent. That means if interest rates go above 9 percent, Pitney receives payments from a bank to fix interest costs at 9 percent. If rates fall below, say, 7 percent, Pitney Bowes pays the bank. By doing this, the company avoids paying an option premium and protects itself against rising interest rates. The company has made use of a $100 million medium-term note (MTN) program that allows it to opportunistically take advantage of favorable medium-term financing rates.

Pitney Bowes continues to create new hedging solutions as its operations have grown. After all, part of the company's overseas strategy is to benefit from the European Economic Community's "1992" plan. The company recently purchased a dealership in Italy. Further it started marketing its postage meters in France where it also acquired a finance company. As a result, it now has direct sales and service operations in the five EEC nations that represent 80 percent of the potential market for its products.

In this interview, both Adimando and Abate explain why financial risk management and innovative funding strategies are a key part of the company's attempt to lower the costs of capital and sales and to maximize the dollar-value inherent in its overseas sales.

Interview: Carmine F. Adimando and Mary Jo Abate

How did you persuade Pitney Bowes' board of directors to take a strategic view on the interrelationship between funding activities and operational competitiveness?

Adimando: I took them through the cost of capital concepts and capital pricing model developed by Bill Sharpe of Stanford University. I showed them how it's calculated for our company and also showed them what the basic cost of capital was for each of our businesses. I got them to look at this company as an overall risk portfolio, with some of these businesses being considered higher risk than others. I then tried to relate that to what happened to the company's stock price over the last four or five years. Overall, we looked at each of our businesses and said, "Here's a business that has a cost of capital of X, and generates returns that aren't significant enough to meet that." We have either got to restructure that business and beef up its returns, or we have to think twice before we put additional investments in those businesses.

To complete my presentation, I took our competitors, looked at their financial statements, and showed management what their cost of capital of was. And in fact, the competitors I showed that had a better cost of capital and better structured balance sheets were also our strongest competitors and highly profitable companies. Why? Because they were therefore able to borrow money or issue equities at a lower cost. This allowed them to gain competitive advantage in terms of pricing and in terms of spending money on R&D. I suggested that we tie in our treasury people to look at what's the best way to finance our companies on a go-forward basis.

At the time, I realized we were eventually going into a borrowing mode here in the U.S., which was basically unheard of at Pitney Bowes. In fact, we did a debt offering in 1987 which was our first debt offering in 19 years, other than for our financial services companies.

Again, certain companies are always in the equity markets, but if you are looking for a company like Pitney Bowes, we hardly ever issued equities per se. The last time was 1981, other than maybe issuing shares for an acquisition. To Pitney Bowes, equity issues traditionally were never vehicles for financing, but cost of capital is a blend of the cost of equity and the cost of debt. As I said, I introduced that concept in 1982 and almost got thrown out of the boardroom by a former chairman. Fortunately, we had some good financiers on our board, and they said, "He's right, we never looked at it that way. Why don't you let him go?" I showed them what our real cost of capital was for the company, how we could leverage up some more and at the same time maintain a good rating with the rating agencies, and how we can take advantage of the risk portfolio of our companies, which at that time were not very risky.

Our only risky business was our copier division, which resembled a high technology company with a beta of 1.5 or 2.0 in 1982. Starting in 1983 and 1984, we calculated cost of capital for every single division and we created hurdle rates for each of them. Based on those hurdle rates, these divisions were expected to give us a return on invested capital commensurate with their risk profile. Each hurdle rate consisted of their cost of capital plus one percentage point to cover corporate expenses, plus two percentage points to ensure an attractive return on investment. When we look at financing new projects or expansions or acquisitions, we calculate the projected return on capital. We put it all together with our debt portfolio and we evaluate what it does to us from a competitive standpoint. Thus, treasury is an integral part of our operations.

Who are your key competitors now, and how does your cost of capital compare to theirs?

Adimando: Since then, our cost of capital has greatly improved. We are leveraged a little bit higher, but the risk portfolio of the company has been lowered. Overall, our beta is lower as a company because of the low-risk nature of our businesses. Other than facsimile and copier businesses, all of our businesses have betas in a range of 1.05 to 1.10 down to as low as 0.80. Fax and copier divisions are probably within the 1.3 to 1.5 range, because that is the competitive nature of those businesses. Overall, we probably run a beta of 1.05 or 1.10. We have been a strong AA-credit for the last couple of years. We put a collar on our leasing companies so that our external leveraging will not grow at the level that it has grown in the last few years. We are targetting our all-in debt to total capital levels at 65 percent. That's a target, which the investors like. We will control that by limiting the amount of new debt on our books—particularly large ticket external leasing business at our financial services businesses. We want to keep our portfolio mix in the proper perspective. We started that in 1988 and have since sold off $400 million worth of external deals. That helped us get our debt ratio down to 66 percent, and our target in the future for the total company is to be at 65 percent or better, with the operating companies being below 30 percent.

With the influence of our board of directors in the 1980s, we were able to convince the operating units that this was how we were going to monitor them. We suggested they also ought to be calculating such numbers themselves, and that they should use these in their own investment analysis. They can now look at their businesses as they stand alones and figure out what kinds of returns their own cost of capital requires. I happen to believe that a company generating returns that are two to three percentage points higher than its cost of capital will continue to attract capital and will be considered in the upper quartile of attractive investments. So that's what we try to do. We provide hurdle rates for our operating units two to three percent above their own cost of capital, and they give us returns matching or exceeding that so that the whole company will generate returns in excess of its cost of capital.

And that's a basic component of the company's strategic plan to remain competitive into the future.

Adimando: Exactly right. We tie our financial planning and operating plans together. One of reasons the board also asked me to assume the responsibility of treasurer is to tie the two together. As a chief financial officer in charge of investor relations, as a senior officer who understands the operational makeup of the company and who has access to planning and development, I am able to drive treasury in that direction. We can then position ourselves within the marketplace and keep our company streamlined against creditors and competitors so that financially there is no strategic disadvantage to Pitney Bowes. As a result, our operating companies can be out there and be armed and dangerous. Their only competition is the quality of their products and services.

Can you explain why interest rate hedging instruments play such an important role in your funding activities?

Adimando: We had a shelf registration coming out in 1990, for example. We checked with the rating agencies to see what their concerns and recommendations were and decided on a shelf of $250 million. We could have gone for as much as $600 million, but operationally a strong credit rating means a lot to us. It may save us 15 or 20 basis points, which means we can come down 20 basis points on our lease rates and be more competitive internally and externally.

If you can save 20 basis points on $2.5 billion dollars of debt, that's significant. Sometimes, we find companies that are strong but can't get good credit ratings; dealing with them, we may be able to do even better than that using swaps or other off balance sheet instruments. Call provisions have also been a way to collect premium to reduce our funding costs. We've been able to swap at very favorable rates with such companies, or with different institutions that know our paper is strong. That's the advantage of being a strong credit. They know we will be there in three years, five years, and ten years.

How does treasury's role in this strategic plan tie into some risk management transactions that you've put together in the past?

Adimando: For one, we obviously have positioned ourselves well with good debt ratings. By having two commercial paper programs— one with First Boston and one with Bank of America—we can finance our day-to-day needs and short- term needs up to one year. While the program with First Boston is our primary program, I also initiated a program with Bank of America because of its retail network and tremendous presence on the West Coast. We wanted that presence with potential shareholders and customers there, and having the paper traded daily there obviously helps. We can then call on these groups as customers for mailing equipment, facsimile equipment, and copy equipment.

Second, we try to position and time the market so that we can issue medium-term notes for our three- to five-year needs, or to look for longer term financing—particulalry with our financial services organizations—to either match portfolios or match transactions. The ideas is to position ourselves so we have blended debt at very favorable rates. Again, this can give us a competitive advantage—or, at least, certainly will not put us at a competitive disadvantage in the marketplace.

This flexibility allows me to go to market when I see the market is favorable to Pitney Bowes, not to wait until there is a transaction that needs financing. At that point, I would be vulnerable to the market's fancy. One of my personal caveats is that I like to borrow at under 9 percent for the operating company. If you go back over the last 15 or 20 years, staying under 9 percent means that you are financing your company securely. That's my caveat on anything beyond our short-term paper needs, and we've done that. We saw some significant windows last year (in 1989), and we put out $50 million in medium-term notes.

That wouldn't haven't been possible without this strategic mindset?

Adimando: Absolutely. We didn't need those notes last year because of our commercial paper program. But if you remember, commercial paper rates shot up to 9 percent in 1989. Therefore, when I saw that window, I realized that I could do some three- and five-year issues. We went out in bits and pieces over a one- to two-month period and locked up 8.45 percent, 8.4 percent, and 8.6 percent. This was

185

significantly better than we could do in the longer term debt markets, which people were hammering. This was 50 to 100 basis points better than I could do with commercial paper when those rates rose.

How did you finance your strategic acquistion of Pandick Technologies?

Adimando: That acquisition gave us a fundamental position in facilities management and repographics management, which is a major strategic objective for our company, which we put forth in the last couple of years. It supplements the business that we created three years ago, and gave us a facility infrastructure in sixteen major cities in the U.S., whereas we were only in two to three cities before. This purchase allows us now to run a significant number of potential customers through these facilities and fully utilize their potential.

To complete this acquisition required that we finance $90 to $100 million at a time when rates weren't favorable. We had been looking at this transaction for four or five months, so finally what I did was place private placement short-term borrowings with a commercial bank that was anxious for our business.

My thinking was to either roll it over until we saw the right window, or supplement that with commercial paper at lower rates and then replace it. If longer term financing rates were better, I would go that route. As it turned out, we rolled it over once. The second time we financed with shorter term paper as long-term rates were blipping up. We saved about 60 basis points doing it that way—by knowing what the markets were doing and knowing that this acquisition was coming. It worked like a charm. We weren't left scratching our heads looking for competitive rates. Here was one of the biggest acquisitions we had made in the last 10 years, and we were able to do it so matter of factly because we had done our homework and fit it into our strategic plan.

Are the off balance sheet markets always in the picture?

Adimando: With the operating companies, we are always looking at swaps and interest rate caps, collars, and floors. Virtually every week, Mary Jo is getting quotes. I am always meeting with investment and commercial bankers myself from a macro standpoint to hear their ideas both from a financing and operating standpoint and a tax standpoint. In fact, some of these ideas that give me significant tax advantages revolve around borrowings.

A good example: we bought the number one office equipment company, Remington Office Products, in Australia to expand our operations. It was being held by a holding company that was having trouble elsewhere and didn't know how to manage this type of company. We made an offer that they accepted after five months of negotiation. In the meantime, I got my tax people and my treasury people togther to meet with a number of financial institutions.

There turned out to be some very favorable tax treaties between Canada and Australia, which go back to World War II. With a cash surplus in Canada that we were having trouble dividending back without paying withholding taxes in the U.S., we acquired the Australian company by creating two shell companies in Canada and the U.S. with very little cash infusion from the U.S. Therefore, I had to borrow very little and had no tax disadvantages. The surplus cash was being generated by an operating division in the international organization, of which the new Australian company was going to be a part. The president of that group was thrilled.

What was the specific tax advantage?

Adimando: The aquisition cost us approximately 20 percent, or C$20 million. There was a minimum withholding tax, in addition to other dividend and tax costs. Thus, we were looking at a savings of $5 to $7 million in taxes and found ourselves with a company generating A$70 to 80 million in one of the largest markets in the world.

Mary Jo, can you explain why active interest rate risk management is important to Pitney Bowes?

Abate: We have started to become a little more active because of acquisitions and R&D. For example, at the end of June 1989, we did a one-year no cost collar on $10 million. If interest rates went over 9.40 or below 7.50, we were covered. We had protection within that range. If they went below, then we would pay the bank. If above, they'd pay us.

We have also used callable swaps in conjunction with debt issues.

So what was the idea behind the callable swap? Is that called a swaption?

Abate: It's sort of a swaption but the option is not my option but the bank's option. Simply put, it's just a swap that is callable in three years.

How much can a corporate save when it sells an option to a bank?

Abate: Quite a bit.

What if rates go lower and you could finance more cheaply without the option?

Abate: We try not to do things all at once. If I had done a $100 million callable swap and that happened, I would probably be a bit upset about it. But on $10 million, that would be fine, because I've got some protection. It's just like the no-cost collar I mentioned. I am most comfortable at certain levels.

From a foreign exchange point of view, is your treasury department centralized or decentralized?

Abate: On the international side, we do everything on a centralized basis, except for the small day-to-day things. The subs can cover those themselves. Any big hedging strategies we do here. We get exposure reports and we also get forecasts quarterly on the rest of the intercompany and third-party payments in different currencies other than their own.

With this information, we then look at the exposures and determine if we want them hedged or not. Each of the subs is responsible for their own P&L. Around September of each year, they usually come in and say, "Next year, we know what we are going to buy from all of the other units, and we would like to lock in our budget." Say it is a British company and they have to sell sterling to buy dollars. They give us the amounts. We look at the forward rates. And we come up with a weighted average for the whole year. Let's say that we can give them an average rate for the whole year of 1.63. That's their rate for every month the entire year. They don't have to change it. But I look at that and say, "Today might be a good day to sell some of it, but I don't want to do the whole year because I would have some gains and some losses because of the averaging." So I may decide to do something else. When the points are against me I might hold it and wait for a more opportune time. They may come in on a Friday and I may want to do something with it the following week. Or if I know the trade numbers are coming out, and I think they will be favorable, I may wait. But if I think they picked a real good time, I may just cover then. But I decide when I cover with the banks and operate as the bank for all the subs.

What are you trying to do with your foreign exchange exposures?

Adimando: Obviously, we don't speculate. What we try to do is eliminate having operating people out in our satellite operations dealing with this problem. For one, they don't have the expertise, and even if they did, it may not fit into what we are doing globally.

189

So, what we have done is take all of our treasury responsibilities from our foreign operations. We do give them operating responsibilities from the standpoint of watching cash flow, monitoring receivables, garnering local investments, and evaluating their local investment requirements, but everything else is handled here including risk management, insurance, and corporate purchasing. We try to set up worldwide contracts, with vendors, and of course, local treasury operations for hedging. Now, in order to make life easy for them, we create budgetted rates every year. We will go out, and Mary Jo and our people will canvas what we feel are the best ten or twelve economists, and we will get their projections—where they see various country economies going, and where they see exchange rates going for the next year and the next five years.

In our planning process, we will take our next year's projections and come up with a range of where we think those currencies will trade vis-à-vis the dollar and vis-à-vis other currencies. We will then set rates on the conservative side, probably toward the lower level, which means the weaker dollar level.

This does two things for us. One, it forces the operating units to struggle to come up with an acceptable budget based on a stronger local currency. Whichever way we go, we lean towards making them struggle towards meeting their budgetted targets.

Which, I suppose, ties into your 2 to 3 percent return caveat?

Adimando: Correct. At that point, they get a budgetted rate. So that's what they are booking month to month without having to worry where the markets are going. The only input that they would have is if they are purchasing from here or from different countries such as Japan, we would want projections on the levels of purchasing they want to make. We then would either suggest hedging that purchase or not and ask them for their decision. They have the option to say: "Yes, we would want to hedge".

Mary Jo and I then would decide ourselves. And this is where

Mary Jo has discretion, because I give her a bogey with which to work. She decides whether we think the rates will get better for Pitney Bowes. If they want to hedge, we will give them a contract at that rate that we've agreed on, whatever it is, and it is usually favorable to their budgetted rate. If they want to lock in, it is usually because they feel they can meet their budget and operate competitively at that rate.

If we feel the markets will get better, we will give them an internal hedge by signing a corporate agreement with them. If we feel that's probably as good a rate as we can get, or we are just not sure how rates will go, we will go out externally and lock that rate up. When we go external, we do a net position. That unit might be a net borrower or might be purchasing from the U.S., and we might have another unit within that same time frame that would be selling to the U.S. So we would look at a net sterling position for the month of June, and say "OK, we are not sure where rates are going to go, but one unit wants to hedge, and the other doesn't want to, so we will go out and lock up that net position." We will give them an internal hedge that will net out to that position.

What is your foreign exchange charter and how are you structured?

Abate: We are not a profit center. We are here just to minimize risk. We are not trying to second guess the operating units. But if they come in on a Friday afternoon and the markets are thin, I may not want to trade at that point. I'll wait for a more opportune time. Since I'm giving an average for the entire year, there are some months that I would be forced to cover at a loss if I simply took the rate I gave them. So I try not to cover anything at a loss—even if it's just a very small gain, or break even, that's OK. I just trying to maximize the opportunities for the company.

We did close to $400 million in foreign exchange last year, so it is nothing like the Kodaks, the Texacos, and a lot of other companies. The principal currencies we deal in are yen, sterling, and the Canadian dollar. The yen is for third-party external contracts since we buy equipment from Japan. Now on those, the operating units may come in and say that they want to cover today. Once again, we ask—is it a good decision or not? With our market knowledge, we are trying to make a sound business decision.

Tell me about your netting system.

Abate: We have a netting system in Amsterdam. Each of the operating units notifies us and also the bank each month of whom they owe, the amount of each currency, and it is all netted. The bank then notifies them of how much they have to pay or receive in their own currency. Normally, because we have all of these internal contracts, we also submit information and say, "They owe us dollars and we owe them sterling." Most of our positions have been covered at this point, unless they forecasted poorly or their requirements grew and they required much more than they thought they would need. Our netting bank will then go out and buy or sell the difference. That's where the bulk of all the transactions that I handle come—through the guaranteed rate system and through the netting system.

Does that mean 90 percent of your transactions are totally hedged?

Abate: No, that is just internal. We also have external positions. Some of those we hedge and some of them we don't. We have quite a few that are not hedged, but I don't know that I could give you a percentage on that.

So with the internal hedges, you are almost operating as a bank.

Adimando: Yes. The bogey I set for Mary Jo is within certain parameters, so that as long as she feels the net exposure is within those given parameters, she can then work either given internally or externally. If it goes beyond that, then she should lock up enough to keep her exposure within that limit, or she should come to me. We would then sit down and agree on what our market position is before we take that risk. Otherwise, she has daily and weekly exposure levels she works with. She has been very good, so we've been on the positive side of this equation. But we don't allow the units to make that decision independently.

If you were to pick your best two or three hedges, Mary Jo, what would those be?

Abate: I can't pick a deal per se. In general, I would say our management of the exposures has been very good. One hedge we are particularly proud of was a dividend hedge. We had had a lot of money in the U.K. and Switzerland for a long time, waiting to get it out. For 1988 and 1989, we took it out at the end of the year. That was when sterling was at its strongest both times. This saved us in excess of $18 million.

So you just locked in with a forward?

Abate: Right.

How is your success measured when you are reviewed? How do they supervise you?

Abate: I report to Carm [Adimando]. It's not based on how much money I made on foreign exchange. It's based on how I have managed things domestically and internationally.

What are the key concerns of your subsidiaries?

Abate: We evaluate how exchange risk impacts our bottom line, so they are very concerned about exposures and how they impact their cost of sales because they are buying from other units outside of their own country.

So you are giving them advice as well?

Abate: Constantly. Constantly. They call and ask, "I need to lock up a budget for next year, should I hedge, should I lock up my cost of sales? What are the rates?"

Carm, how does the strategic point of view that you have talked about tie into Pitney Bowes foreign exchange risk management program?

Adimando: As I said, we buy facsimile machines and copiers from Japan. We don't produce them. Fortunately, in the case of facsimile, everybody buys from Japan. So nobody has a competitive advantage to us vis-à-vis currency exchange rates, unless they've locked it up when we haven't locked it up, and the currency fluctuates drastically. But everybody has the same exposure to the yen fluctuations that we do with facsimile.

In copiers, it's virtually the same, except for Xerox, which manufacturers in the U.S. Other than that, everybody else is using foreign copiers so they will have exposure. If the yen strengthens, it's costing them more to buy facsimile and copiers. When the yen weakens, they are all paying less. We believe, because we have an outstanding service and sales organization, that we bring that to the marketplace better than anybody else. That's our operating advantage. That's our added value. Therefore, whenever we can lock up some favorable currency to what we believe our budget is, and of course our budget rate is an acceptable operating level target, we think it gives us an additional competitive advantage and that we can go in there and get closer to our competitors on price.

Typically, our competitors are probably priced less than us, because all they are doing is selling pieces of equipment, rather than providing significant service. We know that the Japanese companies that are selling in the U.S. don't have the service and sales organization that we have. We have the outstanding distribution network.

Thus, we feel that quantity purchases come to us not just based on price. They come to us because of quality and service as well.

Say IBM buys 1,000 facsimile machines from us, and places them in Fargo, North Dakota; Portland, Oregon; and Tampa, Florida. We can service all those cities. IBM does not want to buy from a company that only has service in three of the fifty cities in which IBM is placing facsimile machines. So they are willing to pay a higher price, but they want those machines to run. To the extent that our higher price can be reduced closer to our competitors, that gives us another advantage with those customers.

You are not trying to be the lowest cost producer, in other words.

Adimando: No. When we manufacturer, we like to be the lowest cost producer with the highest quality. But in OEM purchases, we feel that with all our competition, we still have a distinct advantage in distribution. Thus, we go for product quality and good sourcing first, and then we drive price down by buying in quantitities. For example, in 1990 we started locking up at 150 yen or better for copiers, facsimile machines, and dictation products, so we have locked up anywhere from a 7 percent to 10 percent price advantage versus our budget for those products. Of course, our operating units should meet our targets at budget exchange levels, so therefore, with the hedge, they can do that much more favorably. They have a built in profit and competitive advantage in the market.

Do you have a specific spread at which you are trying to price yourselves relative to your competitors?

Adimando: No. It's all by product and by market—which segment we are selling the product into. We would be in the medium to upper end with all of our products.

In terms of fax and copiers, how has Pitney Bowes done relative to Xerox?

Adimando: Facsimile is a tremendous success story. We have been in the business only seven years, and we are now the number one purchaser of facsimiles in the world. We have made tremendous inroads, exceeding $200 million in worldwide revenues in 1989. From zero, we went to $200 million. Remember, the price of faxes are coming down, and they are getting more feature rich. Copiers are a very competitive business. We only sell in certain segments and try not be a full line supplier. We sell the medium to low upper end machines. That's where we are trying to focus our market. We are not going to the real high end, where the large duplicators are, such as Kodak and Xerox products.

So the copiers and faxes are to maintain your service position that you have developed with customers? For example, if XYZ Corp. started putting all these business machines in your customers' offices, then they might be able to do the same, in terms of mail postage machines, and all of that.

Adimando: That's right. And competitively, in the postage meter business, our competitors are all foreign. There is no U.S. competitor in postage meters.

Who are those competitors?

Adimando: Hasler in Switzerland, Alcatel in France, Postalia in Germany. I guess those are the three majors.

And how has Pitney Bowes done in terms of penetrating their markets?

Adimando: Worldwide, we have about 67 percent of the world-wide postage meter market. We have about 90 percent in the U.S. and Canada, about 60 percent in the U.K., only about 15 percent in Germany, and a nominal presence in France. We hope the latter figures will increase with 1992. We feel we will be very competitive and that those markets will open up for us.

With the postage machine, do you try to maintain service so you can charge a higher price? Or do you have to be very price sensitive?

Adimando: You can only rent postage meters in the U.S., unlike non-U.S. markets. For security purposes, the U.S. Post Office does it that way. The Post Office requires us to inspect the meters every year. We have focused on businesses of five to 50 people in the offices, and we will always be in that market. Those types of companies are price sensitive, but they also won't go back to licking stamps. So what we try to do is put out a reasonable rental cost to them, and at the same time be innovative with leasing our other products. We also introduced postage by phone and are the only company with an electronic meter that has postage by phone in the world. This feature allows you to set your postage by phone without having to go to the post office. Traditionally, you had to go to the post office, give them a check, and they would set the postage for you.

Now you do it by phone. You send us a check, and deposit it into the trust, and a day or two later call up the trust and give us your name. We give you an algorithm to key into the phone and it automatically sets your meter. We have aggressively issued patents around the world on this technology.

We have replenished our meter base with electronic postage by phone. About 40 percent of our customers in the U.S. are using this feature, and we've introduced it in all the other countries. In the production mailing machines area, we are a large competitor of Bell & Howell and some of the European "inserter" companies. We are increasing our sales of shipping and weighing systems, including some very sophisticated systems that help you account for and reduce your postage costs.

Do you hedge on a translation basis at all?

Adimando: No, we do not.

Why?

Adimando: We are in those countries and our units have to exist on that basis. To the extent that we start building surplus cash in those countries and we don't have any local utilization, we will dividend the money out. What I have my tax people doing is looking for opportunities. For example, 1989 was not going to be a year to dividend, so I swept everything out in 1988. We swept accounts out and we took advantage of foreign tax credits. As a result, we paid a minimum amount of tax. For instance, I brought in roughly $60 million dollars net into the U.S. at the peak of exchange for the British pound, Canadian dollar, and Swiss franc. We paid virtually no tax on that—less than $5 million. In 1989, however, had we waited, we would have paid significant amounts of tax.

And why is that?

Adimando: Just because of our ability to use foreign tax credits, of which my tax people were aware. They discussed this with me and my treasury staff. I knew I was going to be dividending out, because I didn't have any investments or acquisitions in the works. By tying that all together, we made a decision that offered significant benefits to the company.

Are you in a unique position as a chief financial officer in the sense that you are hands-on with many of these activities?

Adimando: Yes, I think so. Unfortunately, at other companies, I see CFOs and treasurers that tend to stay in the clouds and let operating people be a little too independent. You must make sure people in treasury are tied into what you are trying to accomplish operationally.

Carm, from a risk management point of view, since you are involved with investor relations, what do you think is important for investors to know about financial risk management? Many still simply consider it speculation.

Adimando: That's true. But in reality, it's strategically driven. The idea is to look at your company's structure, look at your company's cost of capital, and decide what the ideal strategic thrust of your business should be. That is when you will generate the greatest competitive advantages.

Abate: In the past, before this program was developed, there were a lot of opportunity losses. Now, we are actually having some gains each year. We compare what we have done relative to if we had covered when the subs covered, and we have been in a plus position for the last three years. We are simply maximizing our potential opportunities.

11

Merck & Co.*

For the pharmaceutical industry, however, the pricing environment is such that competitive exposure to exchange fluctuations is generally not significant. The existence of price controls throughout most of the world generally reduces a company's ability to react to economic changes. Hence, Merck's exposure to exchange tends to be limited primarily to net asset and revenue exposures. The potential loss in dollar value of net revenues earned oveseas represents the company's most significant economic and financial exposure.

—Judy C. Lewent,
   Vice President and Treasurer
   Merck & Co.

—A. John Kearney,
   Assistant Treasurer
   Merck & Co.

*by **Judy C. Lewent** and **A. John Kearney,** Merck & Co.

Judy Lewent and John Kearney are vice president and treasurer, and assistant treasurer, respectively, of Merck & Co., Inc. Ms. Lewent has spent nine years at Merck and Mr. Kearney has been with the company 20 years.

The authors would like to thank Francis H. Spiegel, Jr., senior vice president and CFO of Merck & Co., Inc., and Professors Donald Lessard of M.I.T. and Darrell Duffie of Stanford for their guidance.

Figure 11.1 Performance in Review:
Merck & Co. (1980–1989)

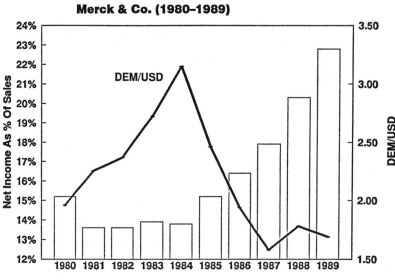

Identifying, Measuring, and Hedging Currency Risk at Merck

The impact of exchange rate volatility on a company depends mainly on the company's business structure, both legal and operational, its industry profile, and the nature of its competitive environment. This chapter recounts how Merck assessed its currency exposures and reached a decision to hedge those exposures. After a brief introduction to the company and the industry, we discuss our methods of identifying and measuring our exchange exposures, the factors considered in deciding whether to hedge such risks, and the financial hedging program we put in place.

An Introduction to the Company

Merck & Co., Inc. primarily discovers, develops, produces, and distributes human and animal health pharmaceuticals. It is part of a global industry that makes its products available for the prevention, relief, and cure of disease throughout the world. Merck is a multinational company, doing business in over 100 countries.

Total worldwide sales in 1989 for all domestic and foreign research-intensive pharmaceutical companies were projected to be $103.7 billion. Worldwide sales for those companies based in the U.S. were projected at $36.4 billion—an estimated 35 percent of the world pharmaceutical market; and worldwide sales for Merck in 1989 were $6.6 billion. The industry is highly competitive, with no single company holding over 5 percent of the worldwide market. Merck ranks first in pharmaceutical sales in the U.S. and the world, yet has only a 4.7 per-cent market share worldwide. The major foreign competitors for the domestic industry are European firms and emerging Japanese companies.

Driven by the need to fund high-risk and growing research expenditures, the U.S. pharmaceutical industry has expanded significantly more into foreign markets than has U.S. industry as a whole. In 1987, the leading U.S. pharmaceutical companies generated 38 percent of their sales revenues overseas, and 37 percent of their total assets were located outside the U.S. In contrast, most U.S. industry groups report foreign sales revenues in the range of 20 percent to 30 percent. Merck, with overseas assets equal to 40 percent of total and with roughly half of its sales overseas, is among the most internationally-oriented of U.S. pharmaceutical companies.

The U.S. pharmaceutical industry also differs from other U.S. multinational companies in its method of doing business overseas. In contrast to U.S. exporters, who often bill their customers in U.S. dollars, the pharmaceutical industry typically bills its customers in their local currencies. Thus, the effect of foreign currency fluctuations on the pharmaceutical industry tends to be more immediate and direct.

Table 11.1   Performance in Review: Merck & Co.
Income Statement (U.S. Dollars in Millions)

	1980	1981	1982	1983	1984
+ Sales	$2,734	$2,930	$3,063	$3,246	$3,560
– Cost of Goods Sold	($1,985)	($2,232)	($2,313)	(2,3899)	($2,613)
Gross Profit	$749	$697	$750	$857	$947
Gross Profit %	27.4%	23.8%	24.5%	26.4%	26.6%
– Depreciation	($91)	($105)	($121)	($135)	($152)
– Other Income & Costs	($5)	($6)	($26)	($23)	($7)
PBT	$652	$586	$604	$698	$789
– Taxes	($237)	($187)	($187)	($247)	($297)
Taxes %	-36.3%	-32.0%	-31.0%	-35.4%	-37.7%
Net Income	$416	$398	$417	$451	$491
Net Income %	15.2%	13.6%	13.6%	13.9	13.8%
Working Capital	$824	$745	$860	$735	$1,077
Working Capital/Sales %	30.1%	25.4%	28.1%	22.6%	30.2%
Long-term Debt	$211	$241	$337	$386	$179
Long-term Debt/Sales %	7.7%	8.2%	11.0%	11.9%	5.0%
Earnings Per Share	$0.92	$0.89	$0.94	$1.02	$1.12
Cash Flow Per Share	$1.13	$1.13	$1.21	$1.32	$1.49
Average Annual P/E	13.2	16.2	13.7	14.9	13.2

1985	1986	1987	1988	1989	Average	CAGR %
3,548	$4,129	$5,061	$5,940	$6,551	$4,076	10.2%
($2,544)	($2,894)	($3,482)	($3,867)	($4,094)	($2,841)	8.4%
$1,004	$1,235	$1,579	$2,073	$2,456	$1,235	14.1%
28.3%	29.9%	31.2%	34.9%	37.5%	29.1%	3.5%
($164)	($194)	($210)	($205)	($222)	($160)	10.4%
$16	$34	$35	$1	($45)	$6	
$856	$1,075	$1,405	$1,869	$2,280	$1,081	14.9%
($317)	($398)	($499)	($664)	($787)	($382)	14.3%
-37.0%	-37.0%	-35.5%	-35.5%	-34.5%	-35.2%	-0.6%
$539	$677	$906	$1,206	$1,494	$699	15.3%
15.2%	16.4%	17.9%	20.3%	22.8%	16.3%	4.6%
$1,107	$1,094	$798	$1,480	$1,503	$1,022	6.9%
31.2%	26.5%	15.8%	24.9%	22.9%	25.8%	-3.0%
$171	$168	$167	$143	$118	$212	-6.3%
4.8%	4.1%	3.3%	2.4%	1.8%	6.0%	15.0%
$1.26	$1.62	$2.23	$3.05	$3.78	$1.68	17.0%
$1.67	$2.13	$2.83	$3.56	$4.34	$2.08	16.1%
14.5	19.8	25.2	18.0	18.6	16.7	3.9%

The typical structure is the establishment of subsidiaries in many overseas markets. These subsidiaries, of which Merck has approximately 70, are typically importers of product at some stage of manufacture, and are responsible for finishing, marketing, and distribution within the country of incorporation. Sales are denominated in local currency, and cost in a combination of local currency (for finishing, marketing, distribution, administration, and taxes), and in the currency of basic manufacture and research—typically, the U.S. dollar for U.S.-based companies.

Identification and Measurement of Exposure

It is generally agreed that foreign exchange fluctuations can affect a U.S. company's economic and financial results in three ways:

1. By changing the dollar value of net assets held overseas in foreign currencies (known as "translations" exposures) or by changing the expected results of transactions in non-local currencies ("transaction" exposures).

2. By changing the dollar value of future revenues expected to be earned overseas in foreign currencies ("future revenue" exposures).

3. By changing a company's competitive position—for example, a competitor whose costs are denominated in a depreciating currency will have greater pricing flexibility and thus a potential competitive advantage ("competitive" exposures).

Competitive exposures have been the subject of much of the recent academic work done on exchange risk management. Such exposures are best exemplified by the adverse affect of the strong dollar on the competitive position of much of U.S. industry in the early 1980s. This was true not only in export markets but also in the U.S. domestic market, where the strengthening U.S. dollar gave Japanese and European-based manufacturers a large competitive advantage in dollar terms over domestic U.S. producers.

For the pharmaceutical industry, however, the pricing environment is such that competitive exposure to exchange fluctuations is generally not significant. The existence of price controls throughout most of the world generally reduces a company's ability to react to economic changes. Hence, Merck's exposure to exchange tends to be limited primarily to net asset and revenue exposures. The potential loss in dollar value of net revenues earned oveseas represents the company's most significant economic and financial exposure. Such revenues are continuously converted into dollars through interaffiliate merchandise payments, dividends, and royalties, and are an important source of cash flow for the company. To the extent the dollar value of these earnings is diminished, the company suffers a loss of cash flow—at least over the short term. And, as discussed in more detail later, the resulting volatility in earnings and cash flow could impair the company's ability to execute its strategic plan for growth.

With its significant presence worldwide, Merck has exposures in approximately 40 currencies. As a first step in assessing the effect of exchange rate movements on revenues and net income, we constructed

Exhibit 11.1 Merck Sales Index

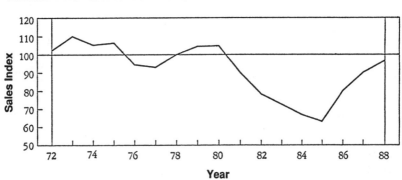

Exhibit 11.2 Merck Sales Index 1978–100%

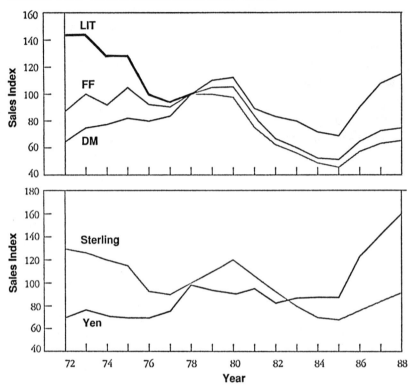

a sales index that measures the relative strength of the dollar against a basket of currencies weighted by the size of sales in those countries.[1] When the index is above 100 percent, foreign currencies have strengthened versus the dollar, indicating a positive exchange effect on dollar revenues. When the index is below 100 percent, as was the case through most of the 1980s, the dollar has strengthened versus the foreign currencies, resulting in income statement losses due to exchange rates.

As Exhibit 11.1 illustrates, the index was relatively stable from 1972 to 1980. But, as the dollar strengthened in the early 1980s, the

Exhibit 11.3 Merck's Geographic Mix of Sales and Assets

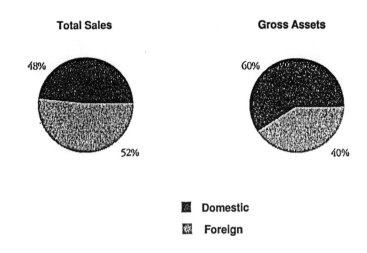

Total Sales   Gross Assets

48%   60%

52%   40%

■ Domestic
▨ Foreign

index declined to the 60 percent level, resulting in a cumulative ex-change reduction in sales of approximately $900 million. But, then, as the dollar weakened in the later 1980s, the index increased to roughly 97 percent, returning to its 1972-1980 range.

But, as Exhibit 11.2 also shows, although the overall index re-turned as of 1988 to the earlier range, not all currencies have moved together against the dollar. The strengthening in the yen and the Deutsche mark has offset the decline of historically weaker currencies such as the Italian lira and French franc, while the British pound is very near 1978 levels.

Given the significant exchange exposure of our net overseas rev-enues, as reflected by our experience in early 1980s, we next decided to review the company's global allocation of resources across curren-cies and, in the process, to determine the extent to which revenues and costs were matched in individual currencies. Our analysis (the main findings of which are illustrated in Exhibit 11.3) revealed that the distribution of Merck's assets differs somewhat from the sales mix, primarily because of the concentration of research, manufacturing, and headquarters operations in the U.S.

On the basis of this analysis, it was clear that Merck has an exchange rate mismatch. To reduce this mismatch, we first considered the possibility of redeploying resources in order to shift dollar costs to a different currency. This process would have involved relocating manufacturing sites, research sites, and employees such as headquarters and support staff. We soon reached the conclusion, however, that because so few support functions seemed appropriate candidates for relocation, a move would have had only a negligible effect on our global income exposure. In short, we decided that shifting people and resources overseas was not a cost-effective way of dealing with our exchange exposure.

Hedging Merck's Exposures with Financial Instruments

Having concluded that resource deployment was not an appropriate way for Merck to address exchange risk, we considered the alternative of financial hedging. Thinking through this alternative involved the following five steps:

1. **Exchange Forecasts.** Review of the likelihood of adverse movements.

2. **Strategic Plan Impact.** Quantification of the potential impact of adverse exchange movements over the period of the plan.

3. **Hedging Rationale.** Critical examination of the reasons for hedging (perhaps the most important part of the process).

4. **Financial Instruments.** Selection of which instruments to use and how to execute the hedge.

210

5. **Hedging Program.** Simulation of alternative strategies to choose the most cost-effective hedging strategy to accommodate our risk tolerance profile (an ongoing process supported by a mathematical model we have recently developed to supplement our earlier analysis).

Step 1:
Projecting Exchange Rate Volatility

Our review of the probability of future exchange rate movements was guided by four main considerations:

(1) The major factors expected to affect exchange rates over the strategic plan period—for example, the U.S. trade deficit, capital flows, the U.S. budget deficit—all viewed in the context of the concept of an "equilibrium" exchange rate.

(2) Target zones or government policies designed to manage exchange rates. To what extent will government policies be implemented to dampen exchange rate volatility, particularly "overshooting" in the future?

(3) Development of possible ranges for dollar strength or weakness over the planning period.

(4) Summary of outside forecasters—a number of forecasters were polled on the outlook for the dollar over the plan period. Our review of outside forecasters showed they were almost evenly split on the dollar's outlook. Although almost no one predicted a return to the extremes of the early 1980s, we nonetheless concluded that there was a potential for a relatively large move in either direction. We developed a simple method for quantifying the potential ranges that reflects the following thought process:

Exhibit 11.4 Probabilities of 20% Movement Per Year

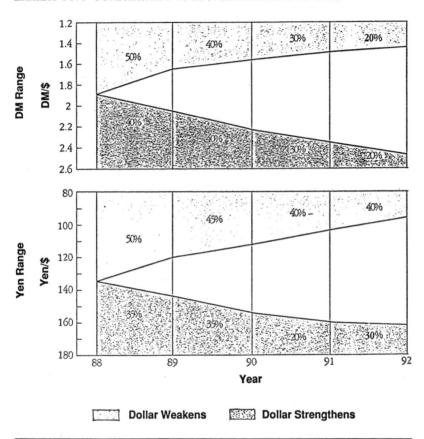

• Except for 1986, the upper limit of the year-to-year movement in average exchange rates for the Deutsche mark and
the yen has been about 20 percent. We used this as the
measure of potential volatility in developing the probabi-
listic ranges in the forecast. (The Deutsche mark, inciden-
tally, was used as a proxy for all European currencies.)

212

- The widest ranges would likely result from one-year directional movements—that is, five years of continued strengthening or weakening.

- However, as the effect of each year's movement is felt in the economy and financial markets, the probability of exchange rates movements continuing in the same direction is lessened. For example, if the dollar were to weaken, the favorable effects on trade balance and on relative asset values would likely induce increased capital flows and cause a turnaround.

Based in part on this concept of exchange rate movements as a "mean-reverting" process, we developed ranges of expected rate movements (as shown in Exhibit 11.4) by assigning probabilities to the dollar continuing to move along a line of consecutive years' strengthening or weakening. For example, the dollar was considered to have

Exhibit 11.5 Unhedged Net Income (1989–1992)

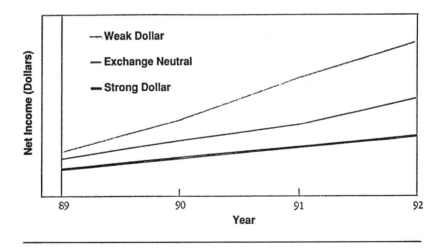

Exhibit 11.6 Exchange Impact Strong Dollar Scenario

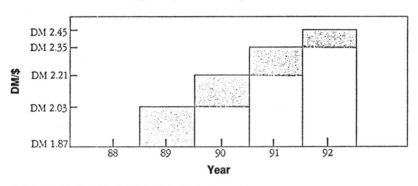

Total bar represents cumulative exchange impact. Shaded area represents year-on-year impact.

a 40 percent probability of strengthening by 20 percent versus the DM in 1989. If the dollar does appreciate by 20 percent in 1989, then we also assume that the probability of its strengthening by a further 20 percent in 1990 is also 40 percent, but that the chance of this pattern continuing in 1991 is only 30 percent and falls to 20 percent in 1992.

Such ranges represent our best guess about the likely boundaries of dollar strength or weakness. The actual probability of exchange rate movements reaching or exceeding those boundaries is small, but the use of such extreme rates allows us to estimate the extent of our exposure. These exchange boundaries were also used in quantifying the potential impact of unfavorable exchange rate movements on our Strategic Plan.

Step 2:
Assessing the Impact on the
5-year Strategic Plan

To assess the potential effect of unfavorable exchange rates, we converted our Strategic Plan into U.S. dollars on an exchange neutral basis (that is, at the current exchange rate) and compared these cash basis (that is, at the current exchange rate) and compared these cash flow and earnings projections to those we expected to materialize under both our strong dollar and weak dollar scenarios. (See Exhibit 11.5.)

Further, we measured the potential impact of exchange rate movements on a cumulative basis as well as according to the year-to-year data that is standard in external reporting. Exhibit 11.6 shows the effect of translating the year-to-year data from Exhibit 11.5 on a cumulative basis. (The total bar represents the cumulative variance, while the top portion represents the variance as determined by the change in rates from one period to the next.) Because it looks beyond a one-year period, the cumulative exchange variance provides a more useful estimate of the size of the exchange risk associated with Merck's long-range plan. Use of a cumulative measure also provides the basis for the kind of multi-year financial hedging program that, as we eventually determined, is appropriate for hedging multi-year income flows.

Step 3:
Deciding Whether to Hedge
the Exposure

Over the long term, foreign exchange rate movements have been—and are likely to continue to be—a problem of volatility in year-to-year earnings rather than one of irreversible losses. For example, most of the income statement losses of the early 1980s were recouped in the following three years. The question of whether or not to hedge exchange risk thus becomes a question of the company's own risk profile with respect to interim volatility in earnings and cash flows.

The desirability of reducing earnings volatility due to exchange rate volatility can be examined from both external and internal perspectives.

External Concerns. These center on the perspective of capital markets, and, accordingly, involve matters such as share price, inves-

Exhibit 11.7 Trade Weighted Dollar Versus Drug Index

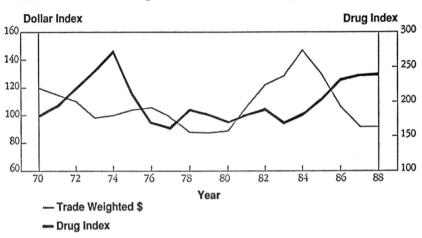

tor effects, and maintenance of dividend policy. Although exchange fluctuations clearly can have material effects on reported accounting earnings, it is not clear that exchange-related fluctuations in earnings have significant effects on stock prices. Our own analysis (as illustrated in Figure 11.7) suggests only a modest correlation in recent years between exchange gains and losses and share price movements, and a slight relationship in the strong dollar period—the scenario of greatest concern to us.

Industry analysts' reports, moreover, tend to support our analysis by arguing that exchange gains and loses are at most a second-order factor in determining the share prices of pharmaceutical companies. While invariably stressing the importance of new products as perhaps the most critical share price variable, analysts also often comment on the regulated price environment overseas (which, as we pointed out earlier, limits competitive exposure by reducing the effect of exchange changes on sales volume).[2]

With respect to investor clientele, exchange would seem to have mixed effects. To the extent that some investors—especially overseas investors—see Merck's stock as an opportunity for speculating on a weak dollar, hedging would be contrary to investors' interests. But, for investors seeking a "pure play" on the stocks of ethical drug companies, significant exchange risk could be undesirable. Thus, given this potential conflict of motives among investors, and recognizing our inability to ascertain the preferences of all of Merck's investors (potential as well as current), we concluded that it would be inappropriate to give too much weight to any specific type of investor.

On the issue of dividend policy, we came to a somewhat different conclusion. Maintaining Merck's dividend, while probably not the most important determinant of our share price, is nevertheless viewed by management as an important means of expressing our confidence in the company's prospective earnings growth. It is our way of reassuring investors that we expect our large investment in future research (funded primarily by retained earnings) to provide requisite returns. And, although both Merck and the industry in general were able to maintain dividend rates during the strong dollar period, we were concerned about the company's ability to maintain a policy of dividend growth during a future dollar strengthening. Because Merck's (and other pharmaceutical companies') dividend growth rates did indeed decline during the strong dollar 1981–1985 period, the effect of future dollar strengthening on company cash flows could well constrain future dividend growth. So, in considering whether to hedge our income against future exchange movements, we chose to give some weight to the desirability of maintaining growth in the dividend.

In general, then, we concluded that although our exchange hedging policy should consider capital market perspectives (especially dividend policy), it should not be dictated by them. The direct effect of exchange fluctuations on shareholder value, if any, is unclear; and, thus, it seemed a better course to concentrate on the objective of maximizing long-term cash flows and to focus on the potential effect of exchange rate movements on our ability to meet our internal objectives. Such actions, needless to say, are ultimately intended to maximize returns for our shareholders.

Internal Concerns. From the perspective of management, two key factors that would support hedging against exchange volatility are as follows: the large proportion of the company's overseas earnings and cashflows; and the potential effect of cash flow volatility on our ability to execute our strategic plan—particularly, to make the investments in R&D that furnish the basis for future growth. The pharmaceutical industry has a very long planning horizon, one which reflects the complexity of the research involved as well as the lengthy process of product registration. It often takes more than 10 years between the discovery of a product and its market launch. In the current competitive environment, success in the industry requires a continuous, long-term commitment to a steadily increasing level of research funding.

Given the cost of research and the subsequent challenges of achieving positive returns, companies such as Merck require foreign sales in addition to U.S. sales to generate a level of income that supports continued research and business operations. The U.S. market alone is not large enough to support the level of our research effort. Because foreign sales are subject to exchange volatility, the dollar equivalent of worldwide sales can be very unstable. Uncertainty can make it very difficult to justify high levels of U.S. based-research when the firm cannot effectively estimate the pay-offs from its research. Our experience, and that of the industry in general, has been that cash flow and earnings uncertainty caused by exchange rate volatility leads to a reduction of growth in research spending.

Such volatility can also result in periodic reductions of corporate spending necessary to expand markets and maintain supportive expenditures. In the early 1980s, for example, capital expenditures by Merck and other leading U.S. pharmaceutical companies experienced a reduction in rate of growth similar to that in R&D.

Our conclusion, then, was that we should take action to reduce the potential impact of exchange volatility on future cash flows. Reduction of such volatility removes an important element of uncertainty confronting the strategic management of the company.

Exhibit 11.8 Alternating Hedging Instruments

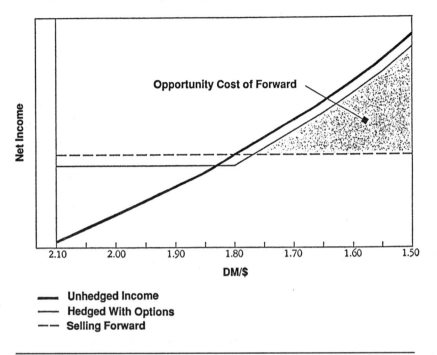

Unhedged Income
Hedged With Options
Selling Forward

Step 4:
Selecting the Appropriate
Financial Instruments

While we will not discuss the various hedging techniques in detail, we do wish to share the thought processes that led us to choose currency options as our risk management tool. Our objective was to select the most cost-effective hedging instrument that accommodated the company's risk preferences.

Forward foreign exchange contracts, foreign currency debt, and currency swaps all effectively fix the value of the amount hedged regardless of currency movements. With the use of options, by contrast, the hedging firm retains the opportunity to benefit from natural positions—albeit at a cost equal to the premium paid for the option. As illustrated in Exhibit 11.8, under a strong dollar scenario (based on 1988 spot rates and forward points), Merck would prefer a forward sale because the contract would product the same gains as the option but without incurring the cost of the option premium. But, under the weak dollar scenario, both the unhedged and the option positions would be preferred to hedging the forward contract.

Given the possibility of exchange rate movements in either direction, we were unwilling to forgo the potential gains if the dollar weakened; so options were strictly preferred. We also concluded, moreover, that a certain level of option premiums could be justified as the cost of an insurance policy designed to preserve our ability to carry through with our strategic plan.[3]

Step 5:
Constructing a Hedging Program

Having selected currency options as our hedging vehicle and designated the 5-year period of our strategic plan as our hedging horizon, we then considered several implementation strategies, including:

- **Varying the term of the hedge.** That is, using year-by-year rather than multi-year hedging.

- **Varying the strike price of the foreign exchange options.** For example, out-of-the-money options were considered as a means of reducing costs.

- **Varying the amount.** That is, different percentages of income could be covered, again, to control costs.

After simulating the outcome of alternative strategies under various exchange rate scenarios, we came to the following decisions: (1) we would hedge for a multi-year period, using long-term options to protect our strategic cash flow; (2) we would not use far-out-of-the-money options to reduce costs; and (3) we would hedge only on a partial basis and, in effect, self insure for the remainder.

We continue to refine this decision through our use of increasingly more sophisticated modeling. Recognizing this as a quantitative process whereby decisions can be improved by application of better techniques, Merck has been developing (with the guidance of Professor Darrell Duffie of Stanford University) a state-of-the-art computer model that simulates the effectiveness of a variety of strategies for hedging. The model is a Monte Carlo simulation package that presents probability distributions of unhedged and hedged foreign income for future periods (the shortest of which are quarters). By so doing, it allows us to visualize the effect of any given hedging policy on our periodic cash flows, thus permitting better-informed hedging decisions.

The model has six basic components:

1. **Security Pricing Models:** State-of-the-art financial analytics are used to calculate theoretical prices for various securities such as bonds, futures, forwards, and options.[4]

2. **Hedging Policy:** We can specify a variety of hedging policies, with each representing a portfolio of securities to buy or sell in each quarter. The number of hedging policies is essentially unlimited, reflecting a variety of hedge ratios, proxy currencies, accounting constraints, security combinations, etc. For example, the model permits us to compare a hedging program of purchasing options that cover the exposures of the 5-year planning period and holding them until maturity with the alternative of a dynamic portfolio revision strategy. A dynamic hedge would involve not only the initial purchase of options,

but a continuous process of buying and selling additional options based on interim changes in exchange rates.

3. **Foreign Income Generator:** Before simulating changes in hedging policy, however, we start by building our strategic plan forecast of local currency earnings into the model. The model then generates random earnings by quarter according to a specified model of forecast projections and random forecast errors. This process provides us with an estimate of the variability of local currency earnings and thereby allows us to reflect possible variations versus plan forecasts with greater accuracy.

4. **Exchange Rate Dynamics:** The model uses a Monte Carlo simulator to generate random exchange rates by quarter. The simulator allows us to adjust currency volatilities, rates of reversion, long-term exchange rates, and coefficients of correlation among currencies. We can test the sensitivity of the simulator to stronger or weaker dollar exchange rates by modifying the inputs. We can also use the Monte Carlo simulator package to re-examine the development of exchange scenarios and ranges described earlier. [5]

5. **Cash Flow Generator:** The model collects information from each of the above four components so as to calculate total cash flow in U.S. dollars by quarter for each random scenario.

6. **Statistical and Graphical Output:** The quarterly cash flow information for each of a large number of scenarios is collected and displayed graphically in frequency plots, and in terms of statistics such as means, standard deviations, and confidence levels. Exhibit 11.9 provides an example of the graphical output from our simulator, comparing distributions of unhedged and hedged cash flows. In this case, the hedged curve assumes 100

Exhibit 11.9 Merck Foreign Cash Flow Unhedged Versus Hedged

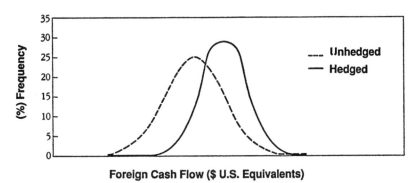

Foreign Cash Flow ($ U.S. Equivalents)

* Hedge of 100% of Cash Flow

percent of Merck's exposure has been covered through the purchase of foreign currency options. Given the pattern of exchange rate movements simulated, the hedging strategy has shifted the hedged cash flow distribution to the right, cutting off a portion of unfavorable outcomes. In addition, the hedged cash flow distribution has a higher mean value as well as a lower standard deviation. Therefore, in this scenario, hedging would be preferable to not hedging, resulting in higher returns as well as lower risk. (Again, of course, the trade-off is the initial cost of option premums that would have to be balanced against the improved risk/return pattern.) Other scenarios may indicate that a lower hedge ratio or not hedging is the preferred strategy.

In sum, the model provides Merck with a powerful tool to determine the optimal strategy for reducing our exposure to foreign currency risk. The simulator allows us to analyze a wide range (in fact, an infinite number) of exchange scenarios, hedging policies, and security combinations. This in turn gives us the ability to select the hedging policy that is both cost-effective and consistent with our desired risk profile.

Conclusion

Indentifying a company's exchange risk and reaching a decision with respect to what action, if any, should be taken requires extensive analysis. We believe that, as a result of this kind of analysis of Merck's currency exposures, we have developed an appropriate financial hedging plan—one that provides management with what amounts to an insurance policy against the potentially damaging effect of currency volatility on the company's ability to carry out its strategic plan. We continue to refine the actual implementation process as we move forward.

Chapter 11 Notes

1. The index uses 1978 as its base year. The currency basket excludes hyperinflationary markets where exchange devaluation is the measured net of price increases.

2. Some analysts have also claimed to detect an inverse relationship between drug stock prices and inflation that also acts to reduce currency exposure. Drug stocks, as this reasoning goes, are growth stocks and generally benefit from low inflation because the discount factor used to price growth stocks declines under low inflation which increases shareholder value. Likewise a high inflation environment will depress share prices for growth stocks. Generally, since high inflation leads to a weaker dollar, the negative impact of high inflation would over time limit the positive effect of a weaker dollar and the reverse would also be true.

3. It was also recognized that to the extent hedge accounting could be applied to purchased options, this represents an advantage over other foreign currency instruments. The accounting ramifications of mark-to-market versus hedge accounting were, and remain, an important issue and we have continued to monitor developments with respect to the ongoing controversy over accounting for currency options.

4. In pricing options, we have the choice of using the Black- Scholes model or an alternative highly advanced valuation model. These models provide reasonably reliable estimates of the expected true cost, including transaction fees, of the option program. Although Black Scholes is the predominant pricing model in pricing many kinds of options, alternative models appear to have an advantage in the pricing of long-dated currency options. Black Scholes implicitly assumes that the volatility of exchange rates grows exponentially with time to maturity. Generally speaking, the further

out the expiry date, the higher the price. The alternative model has a sophisticated approach in its assumption of a dampened exponential relationship between time to maturity, expected volatility, and price. For this reason, in the case of long-dated options, the Black Scholes model generally overstates options prices relative to the alternative model.

5. The model will also have the ability to simulate historic exchange trends. The model will have access to a large database of historic exchange rates. We will be able to analyze the impact of hedging on a selected time period, for example, the strong dollar period of the 1980s. Or, we can have the model randomly select exchange rate movements from a historical period, resulting in a Monte Carlo simulation of that period.

Notes

Chapter 1

According to the Geneva-based trade agency GATT: "Goods Traded Globally Set Record in '89, GATT Says," *Wall Street Journal*, March 23, 1990, p. A38

Plant With a Future: Garnett, N., "Caterpillar Gets Dug in to $2bn Factory Modernization," *Wall Street Journal*, June 6, 1990, p. 14.

In 1986, Sony of Japan: Aggarwal, R. and Soenen, L. A., "Managing Real Changes in Currency Values: The Role of Multinational Operating Strategies," *Columbia Journal of World Business*, 1989, p. 60.

Eastman Kodak's 1988 annual report stated: Eastman Kodak Company 1988 Annual Report, p. 29.

The article on Kodak: Ansberry, C., "Kodak's 1st-Period Net Plunged; Exchange Rates Blamed, Stock Slides," *Wall Street Journal*, May 3, 1989, p. A5.

The foreign exchange skies were quite unfriendly: UAL Corp. 1988 Annual Report, p. 31.

Pan Am Corporation experienced a consolidated net loss: Pan Am Corporation 1988 Annual Report, p. 24.

Texas Air Corporation nearly doubled: Texas Air Corporation 1988 Annual Report, p. 26.

Zenith Electronic Corp.'s second quarter 1989 loss: "Selling Risk Management Concepts," *Corporate Risk Management*, September/October 1989, p. 8.

Honda Motor of Japan reported a drop of 7.8%: Rodger, I. "Big Loss on Currency Hits Honda," *Financial Times*, February 13, 1990, p. 24.

reported annual profits for Unilever: Harris, C., "Unilever Raises Annual Profits 24% to 1.8 bn," *Financial Times,* February 28, 1990 p. 21.

Hoechst earnings: "Hoechst earnings suffer due to strong D-mark": *Financial Times,* April 4, 1990, p. 20.

Drucker's quote: Drucker, P. F., *The New Realities,* Harper and Row: New York, 1989, p. 128.

Milton Friedman stated: Friedman, M. J., "The Case for Flexible Exchange Rates," *Essays in Positive Economics,* University of Chicago Press: Chicago, 1985.

A New York Federal Reserve Bank census found: Frenkel, J. A. and Froot, K. A., "Chartists, Fundamentalists and Trading in the Foreign Exchange Market," *American Economic Review,* May 1990, p. 182.

As the Scottish economist R. MacDonald concluded: MacDonald, R., *Floating Exchange Rates: Theory and Evidence,* Cambridge, Massachusetts: Allen and Unwin, Inc., 1988, p. 295.

the Federal Reserve found that the successful navigation of Japanese automakers: Anderson, G. H. and Carlson, J.B., "Does Dollar Depreciation Matter: The Case of Auto Imports from Japan," *Federal Reserve Bank of Cleveland,* May 1, 1987.

Sony initiated a downsizing program: Aggarwal, R. and Soenen, L. A., "Managing Real Changes in Currency Values: The Role of Multinational Operating Strategies," *Columbia Journal of World Business,* 1989, p. 60–66.

An example of global resource development: Borrus, A., "The Stateless Corporation," *Business Week,* May 14, 1990, p. 101.

A recent study by Richard Baldwin: "The Lure of 1992," *The Economist,* November 18, 1989, p. 77.

"the challenge of responsiveness is exacerbated: Bartlett, C., and Ghoshal, S., *Managing Across Borders,* Brookfield, Vermont: Business Books, 1989.

Chapter 2

The U.S. based pharmaceutical giant earns: Lewent, J. C. and Kearney, A. J., "Identifying, Measuring and Hedging Currency Risk at Merck," *Journal of Applied Corporate Finance*, Winter 1990, pp. 19–28.

concurrent development with multifunctional teams seeks: McEachron, N. B. and Tara, R. A., "Reducing Time to Market," SRI International: Business Intelligence Program, Spring 1990.

Chapter 3

An illustration of this type of market pattern: "Medical and Dental Instruments and Supplies," *U.S. Industry Outlook*, Washington, D.C., 1989.

Chapter 4

In a study on exchange rate responsiveness: Ceglowski, J., "Dollar Depreciation and U.S. Industry Performance," *Journal of International Money and Finance*, Vol. 8, June 1989, pp. 233–252.

Kanebo, the world's largest textile group . . .: Rawsthorn, A., "Kanebo's Struggle for Prosperity," *Financial Times*, April 20, 1990.

Molson, Canada's largest brewer, reported . . .: "Molson to Modernise Chemicals Unit," *Financial Times*, April 3, 1990.

A recent study by Michael Knetter: Knetter, M. M., "Price Discrimination by U.S. and German Exporters," *American Economic Review*, March 1989, pp. 198–210.

A recent study by Froot and Klemperer showed: Froot, K. A. and Klemperer, P.D., "Exchange Rate Pass-Through When Market Share Matters," *American Economic Review*, Vol. 79, No. 4, September 1989, pp. 637–654.

Chapter 5

Caterpillar is a global industry leader: Caterpillar Inc. 1989 Annual Report, p. 2.

A 1982 Harvard Business Review article: Hout, T., Porter, M. E. and Rudden, E., "How Global Companies Win Out," *Harvard Business Review*, September-October 1982, pp. 98–108.

According to Caterpillar's treasurer: Rose, R. L., "Caterpillar Sees Gains in Efficiency Imperiled by Strength of Dollar," *Wall Street Journal*, April 6, 1990, p. A10.

Caterpillar's 1989 Annual Report stated: Caterpillar Inc. 1989 Annual Report, p. 5.

Chapter 6

"Unfortunately, the financial analysis...: Barwise, P., Marsh, P.R., and Wensley, R., "Must Finance and Strategy Clash?", *Harvard Business Review*, September-October 1989, pp. 85–89.

"today's game of global strategy...: Porter, M.E., *Competitive Advantage: Creating & Sustaining Superior Performance*, The Free Press: New York, 1985.

In a recent article on creating organizations that learn....: Kiechel, W., "The Organization that Learns," *Fortune*, March 12, 1990, p. 133.

As London Business School chairman Peter Williamson recently remarked: Editor's Viewpoint, "Management Europe", *Business International*, March 1990, p. 2.

General Patton quote: Patton, G. S., *War As I Know It*, Houghton Mifflin Company: Boston, 1947, p. 251.

Chapter 7

As Benton explains: "Mainframes and Microcomputers: The Industry Turns Upside Down in the 1990s—IBM Erodes; Compaq Gains," by Donald C. Benton, *Goldman Sachs' Investment Research*, January 17, 1990, p. 1–5.

Adds Benton: Ibid. p. 9.

Chapter 8

the experience of Lufthansa: Sponsored supplement to INTERMARKET, November 1986, p. 20 and p. 22

Chapter 9

Merrill Lynch analysts Lucy F. Olwel and Jean L. Queally...said: "Baxter International: Second Quarter EPS; Recovery on Track," by Lucy E. Olwell and Jean L. Queally, Merrill Lynch Capital Markets, Global Research and Economics Group, July 24, 1990, p. 61.

Chapter 11

Merck & Co.: Lewent, J. C. and Kearney, A. J., "Identifying, Measuring and Hedging Currency Risk at Merck," *Journal of Applied Corporate Finance,* Winter 1990, pp 19–28.

Bibliography

While not directly referred to in our book, the authors would like to acknowledge the following as important sources of information that influenced their thinking.

"America's Japanaphobia," *The Economist*, Vol. 313, No. 7628, November 11–17, 1989, p. 15.

Asher, B., "Corporate Hedges Are Getting More Sophisticated," *Business International Money Report*, April 9, 1990, pp. 133–138.

Asher, B., "Why FMC Moved to More Aggressive FX Management," *Cross Rates: Business International*, June 1988.

Balachandra, R., "Winning the Race to the Marketplace," *Wall Street Journal*, April 30, 1990, p. A14.

Baldoni, R., "Managing the Risks," Corporate Finance, February 1990, pp. 43–45.

Benrey, R.M., "Assessing Value-Based Strategic Planning," SRI International: Business Intelligence Program, May 1990.

Bhagwati, J.N., Brecher, R.A. and Hatta, T., "The Global Correspondence Principle: A Generalization," *American Economic Review*, March 1987, pp. 124–132.

Bradshaw, D., "Toshiba's Way to Shrink the Chips," *Financial Times*, April 26, 1990, p. 12.

Celebuski, M. J., Hill, J. M. and Kilgannon, J. J., "Managing Currency Exposures in International Portfolios," *Financial Analysts Journal*, January-February 1990, pp. 16–23.

Chew, L., "Damage Control," *Risk*, April 1988.

Corporate Risk Management Magazine, Official Transcript of Annual Conference on Corporate Risk Management, November 12–14, 1989.

Danker, S., "JAL Sets Course for Private Sector Success," *Risk*, April 1988.

Devlin, G., The Effective Development of Strategic Options, SRI International, February 1990.

"Exposure Management," FFO, Business International, January 1990.

Falloon, W. D., "How Westinghouse Uses One Room for Financial Risk," *Business International Money Report*, July 3, 1989, pp. 205–210.

Feldstein, M. "The Case Against Trying to Stabilize the Dollar," *American Economic Review*, May 1989, pp. 36–40.

Foxen, R. and Wachter, T., "Going Global," SRI International: Business Intelligence Program, Fall 1989.

Frenkel, J. A., "The International Monetary System: Should It Be Reformed?", *American Economic Review*, May 1987, pp. 205–210.

——— and Froot, K. A., "Chartists, Fundamentalists, and Trading in the Foreign Exchange Market," *American Economic Review*, May 1990, pp. 181–185.

——— and Mussa, M. L., "The Efficiency of Foreign Exchange Markets and Measures of Turbulence," *American Economic Review*, May 1986, pp. 374–381.

Gatling, R., "Boosting the Chances of Getting Hedge Accounting Treatment," *Business International Money Report*, March 19, 1990, pp. 106–107.

———, "Seagram: A Long-Term Strategy for Financial Risk Management," *Business International Money Report*, March 12, 1990, pp. 95–98.

———, "Sharing Risk Management with Shareholders," *Business International Money Report*, May 7, 1990, pp. 165-167.

Geanuracus, J., "How Monsanto Hedges Dollar Budget Commitments in Europe," *Business International Money Report*, April 2, 1990, p. 119."

"German Unity Could Mean Extra Taxes," *Business Europe*, February 23, 1990, p. 1.

Golub, S. S., "Foreign Currency Government Debt, Asset Markets and the Balance of Payments," *Journal of International Money and Finance*, Vol. 8, June 1989, pp. 285–294.

Hillman, J., "To the SEC: About Economic Risk...", *Corporate Risk Management*, May/June 1990, p. 46.

Hoare Govett, *World Stock Market Review*, April 6, 1990, p. 38.

Hodrick, R. J., "Volatility in the Foreign Exchange and Stock Markets: Is It Excessive?", *American Economic Review*, May 1990, pp. 186–191.

"How to Handcuff a Central Bank," *The Economist*, May 5, 1990, p. 93.

Hyde, M, *Cemical Insight*, No. 433, March 1990.

Institute for International Research, Official Transcript of Conference on Global Financial Risk Management, June 27–28, 1989.

Isaac, A. G., "Exchange Rate Volatility and Currency Substitution," *Journal of International Money and Finance*, Vol. 8, June 1989, pp. 274–284.

Jonquieres, Guy, "Foreign Investment Changing Structure of World Economy," *Financial Times*, April 9, 1990, p. 3.

Kanabayashi, M., "Weak Yen May Be Steroid for Some Exporters, Japanese Securities Firms' Crystal Ball Shows," *Wall Street Journal*, March 29, 1990, p. C2.

Kazimirski, M., "Hewlett-Packard: Getting Finance Organized for 1992," *Business International Money Report*, February 12, 1990, pp. 53–54.

———, "Nestle: Financial Structure and Foreign Exchange Strategy," *Business International Money Report*, April 30, 1990, p. 159.

Kenen, P. B., "Exchange Rate Management: What Role for Intervention?", *American Economic Review*, May 1987, pp. 194–199.

Krugman, P., "The J-Curve, the Fire Sale, and the Hard Landing," *American Economic Review*, May 1990, pp. 31–35.

——— and Obstfeld, *International Economics: Theory and Policy*, Scott, Foresman and Company: Boston, 1988.

Landau, N., "A Strong Dollar Makes Wall St. Take FX Seriously," *Business International Money Report*, October 30, 1990, pp. 345–346.

235

Landau, N., "Finance: Helping Make MNCs Competitive," *Business International Money Report*, April 2, 1990, p. 125.

Laursen, E., "Carbide and GMAC Find New Ways to Play Interest Rates Overseas," *Corporate Finance*, May 1989, p. 58.

Makin, C., "How to Manage a Global Money Manager," *Institutional Investors*, April 1990, pp. 69–70.

Maloney, P. J., "Managing Currency Exposure: The Case of Western Mining," *Journal of Applied Corporate Finance*, Winter 1990, pp. 29–34.

"Markets," *Forbes*, January 16, 1990, p. 32.

Marsh, D., "Strength of D-Mark Depresses Bayer 3%," *Financial Times*, May 9, 1990, p. 25.

McCauley, D., "How Becton Dickinson Uses Cross-Border Teams to Make 'Transnationalism' Work," *Business International*, February 26, 1990, p. 68.

McKinnon, R. I., "Monetary and Exchange Rate Policies for International Financial Stability: A Proposal," *Journal of Economic Perspectives*, Winter 1988, pp. 83-103.

Meese, R. A., and Rose, A. K., "Nonlinear, Nonparametric, Nonessential Exchange Rate Estimation," *American Economic Review*, May 1990, pp. 192–196.

Melamed, L., editor, *The Merits of Flexible Exchange Rates*, George Mason University Press: Fairfax, Virginia, 1988.

Millman, G. J., "How Smart Competitors Are Locking in the Cheap Dollar," *Corporate Finance*, December 1988, pp. 45–47.

———, "How Westinghouse Invests Its Cash in the Currency Markets," *Corporate Finance*, March 1990, p. 57.

———, "Merck Hedges Currencies to Protect its R&D Budget," *Corporate Finance*, April 1990, pp. 71–73.

———, "Why Multinationals Are Rushing Into Economic Hedging," *Corporate Finance*, February 1990, pp. 51–53.

Neumann, E., "Caterpillar: A Strong Dollar and the Perils of Not Hedging," *Business International Money Report*, February 26, 1990, p. 71.

Ohmae, K., "Toward a Global Regionalism," *Wall Street Journal,* April 27, 1990, p. A10.

Ordover, J. A. and Willig, R. D., "Perspectives on Mergers and World Competition," Princeton University: Discussion Paper No. 88, March 1985.

Port, O., "A Smarter Way to Manufacture," *Business Week,* April 30, 1990, pp. 110–117.

Protecting Profits from Market Turmoil: Strategic Financial Risk Managing for the 1990s, Business International Research Report: New York, 1990.

Rawls, S. W. and Smithson, C. W., "Strategic Risk Management," *Journal of Applied Corporate Finance,* Winter 1990, pp. 6–18.

———, "The Evolution of Risk Management Products," *Journal of Applied Corporate Finance,* Winter 1989, pp. 19–26.

Riddell, P., "S&L Industry Rescue Plan Soars to Between $90bn and $130bn," *Financial Times,* May 24, 1990, p. 18.

Rosenthal, M., "The Organization That Learns," *Fortune,* March 12, 1990, pp. 133–136.

Schreffler, R., "It's Making Our Life Miserable," *Business Week,* May 7, 1990, pp. 48–49.

Sesit, M. R., "Japanese Influence Grows in Global Currency Market," *The Wall Street Journal,* September 14, 1989.

Shapiro, A. C., *Multinational Financial Management* Third Edition, Boston: Allyn and Bacon, 1989.

Sheridan, E., "Hedging Economic Risk," *Corporate Finance,* May 1990.

Smith, C. W., Smithson, C. W. and Wilford, D. S., "Managing Financial Risk," *Journal of Applied Corporate Finance,* Winter 1989, pp. 27–48.

"The Changing Role of the CFO: More Management Tasks, Greater Corporate Visibility," *Business International Money Report,* March 27, 1989, p. 94.

"The World Competitiveness Report," *European Affairs,* Autumn 1989, pp. 114–126.

Yoshikawa, H., "On the Equilibrium Yen-Dollar Rate," *American Economic Review,* June 1990, pp. 576–583.

Index